AN AMERICAN UNCONSCIOUS

MEBANE ROBERTSON

poems

BLACK
WIDOW
PRESS

Boston, MA

AN AMERICAN
UNCONSCIOUS

Joseph S. Phillips and Susan J. Wood, Ph.D., Publishers
www.blackwidowpress.com

Cover Art: Anna Atkins, "Halymenia furcellata," from *Photographs of British algae: cyanotype impressions.* The Digital Collections of The New York Public Library.

Cover Design & Text Production: Kerrie Kemperman

ISBN-13: 978-0-9971725-0-8

Printed in the United States
10 9 8 7 6 5 4 3 2 1

for my father

TABLE OF CONTENTS

PART ONE

Death of a Metronome ~ 15
The Mole Rat ~ 16
Another Opaque Out Trip ~ 18
Mary Morrison ~ 19
Throwing the Thing in Reverse ~ 21
Dunce Years ~ 23
Freshman Rush ~ 25
Kandinsky in Love ~ 26
Driving Out of a Dry County ~ 27
Consolation and Loving Others ~ 28
Before Drifting Off ~ 29
Mr Gomer, or All the Pretty Red Flags ~ 30
Secret Valves, Strong River ~ 32
Playing with Pills ~ 34
James Naylor's Tongue Bore Through ~ 35
And Other Living Things ~ 36
Nick ~ 37
Red Jeep on Edge ~ 38
Angels and Snuff ~ 40
Song of the Sands ~ 41
All We Dig Up ~ 42
That Plane Is Hardly Moving, If At All ~ 43
Says Mr. Richards ~ 45
The Settlement ~ 46
Deeming Where You Are ~ 47
Troubled Insights ~ 48

Manifesto Ostinato ~ 49
Reality Check ~ 51
Throwback Recognition Scene ~ 52
Pinot Noire ~ 53
Why Must It Be This Way ~ 54
Lighted And Laughing ~ 55
Last Clear Chance ~ 56

PART TWO

Moon Apples ~ 59
A Toast for All My Dear Ones ~ 60
Drawing Alone from a Common Spring ~ 61
Last Line of the Blithedale Trilogy ~ 63
The Hat on the Bed ~ 64
The In's and Out's of Adoption (Uriel Angel
    Sanctioned) ~ 65
Alkaline Shine ~ 66
Forever Gone ~ 67
The Safety ~ 68
Recessed Blessings ~ 70
A Hint of Sweet Science ~ 71
Restorative Yoga ("It's a Beautiful Life") ~ 72
Negligent Design ~ 73
The Rushes ~ 74
Byron on the Beach ~ 75
Come Visit, but Don't Stay ~ 76
Take Oasis ~ 77
Just Before Lights Out ~ 78
Took a Blue Canoe ~ 80
You're Very Good At What You Do ~ 81
Mercies ~ 82
One Hour at a Time ~ 83
Dishrag ~ 84
The Only Handwritten One ~ 85

My Job for You to Notice ~ 86
For Granted ~ 87
Now and Always With You ~ 88
Gag Order ~ 89

PART THREE

26th and Atlantic ~ 93
Mr. Very ~ 94
Neighbors ~ 95
Flagging You In ~ 96
Chance Happening ~ 97
The Wecoming ~ 98
Scene from Cortelyou ~ 99
Complaint and Subterfuge ~ 100
Comedy Club ~ 101
Nine Iron ~ 102
A Man in a Certain House ~ 103
Knowing, Not Knowing ~ 104
Minor Alterations ~ 105
Brittle Days, Nervous Nights ~ 106
Only by Proximity ~ 107
This Stupid Dig ~ 108
NYC, Sixteen ~ 109
Everyone's Tired of You ~ 111
Delirium Tremens ~ 112
Well, Well, Well ~ 113
Right Side Out ~ 114
Greeting of the Players ~ 116
June You Were My Desire ~ 117
Mile of Bad Road ~ 118
In the Rising Sun ~ 119
Lines in Braille ~ 120
Petitioning Spiderman ~ 121
On the Advice of a True Friend ~ 122

Snagging a Fly in the Bleachers ~ 123
Lemon Chicken ~ 124
French and English Suites ~ 125
You Who Never Were ~ 126
A Ruined House ~ 127
A Fig Tree Growing Wild ~ 128
A Word from our Sponsors ~ 129
The Steakhouse ~ 130
Rat's Nest ~ 131
Rain in April ~ 133
Morbid Dread ~ 134
A Magical Dream ~ 135
A Place to Be ~ 136
An Occasional Poem ~ 137
Long Look into Night ~ 138
The Fronds ~ 139
Driving Through the Grove ~ 141
Apr 26, '12 ~ 142
Parasite ~ 143
Necessary Conditions ~ 144
After the War ~ 145
The St. Croix Mix ~ 146
Lake by St. Charles ~ 147
Williamsburg ~ 148
A Tree in the Breeze ~ 150
Tenure ~ 151

20.5 POEMS

1 ~ 155
2 ~ 156
3 ~ 157
4 ~ 158
5 ~ 159
6 ~ 160

7 ~ 161
8 ~ 162
9 ~ 163
10 ~ 164
10.5 ~ 165
11 ~ 166
12 ~ 167
13 ~ 168
14 ~ 169
15 ~ 170
16 ~ 171
17 ~ 172
18 ~ 173
19 ~ 174
20 ~ 175

CAREFREE AND COMELY

Rules of Temptation ~ 179
Airport Man ~ 180
Lottery Dunce ~ 181
Valences ~ 182
At Forty ~ 183
Circle of Cats ~ 184
Invite ~ 185
Some Lines Crossed Out ~ 186
Uncontrollable Laughter ~ 187
The Puppy's Tail ~ 188
Worries ~ 189
Green Heights ~ 190
The Speaker Has The House ~ 191
Much Less Forgiven ~ 192
Personality by Committee ~ 193
Letting the Shade Up ~ 194
Today's Mail ~ 195

Three Cents Worth ~ 196
Evident Courage ~ 197
Duck Blind Bourbon ~ 198
Tops ~ 199
A Short Drive ~ 200
Incidental Music ~ 201
The Long and Short of It ~ 202
Mounting Toil ~ 203
The Zoo ~ 204
The Boys Above Are Baffled ~ 205
Simple Pleasures ~ 206
After Long Suffering ~ 207
Off the Ground but Barely ~ 208
Offering of Distraction ~ 209
Various Enclosures ~ 210
Your Turn ~ 211
Blue Lighthouse ~ 212
Your Carryall Bag ~ 213
Red Stringer ~ 214
Listing Breeze ~ 215
Flying on Ether ~ 216
Growth of an English Boxwood ~ 217
Another Bassoon Track ~ 218

PART ONE

DEATH OF A METRONOME

At this time of day, it's hard to know where to begin. The storm
Came up strong in the night and was a beauty, swirling down the
    alley
While I was over at a friend's place in the city.

But from the remnants in twelve-point type, I know it was once
Bonded by a most august consanguinity, mixing iron, blood, and
    wood,
With the spray of the times — self-help manuals and the like.

There are so many approaches you can take — the face with its
Back cut and sheer sheets of ice, for those who like to risk it all,
Or, say, the summer slopes where we share digital cell phone pictures

With our children, dressed — we not the children — in ermine and
    tulle.
We would dance some ancient dance, but the musicians are tapped
    out.
— In their place are the technicians who are to music what a gas

Burning fireplace is to a real flaming roar of fatwood, and
Through our mediums — no, not media — we seed the brain pans
Of the ones we love but whom, for whatever reason, we cannot go to.

By now the surface is all ice, maybe a foot or so thick, so we
Have the metabolism of machines, and the people who cut the holes
Are out with their tackle boxes and flasks of human warmth.

And then there's the mother with the gold patina around her head.
We turn on our pillows and leave our traces forever to call upon her.
This is the crime scene in the day of our vegetable love.

THE MOLE RAT

These hours alone are the other's knowing you are fighting off the
    snake.
They block in the tunnel behind you for the good of the colony.
After all, if the snake were to gain access to the main passageway,
    unspeakable
Carnage would result. So they don't text, don't call. It's you
And the snake — and please don't imbue this with the Garden
    metaphor —
And who's to sink fangs or teeth into the other is really up for grabs.

My money is on you, sitting there with a forty of Malt liquor, too
    proud
To reach out to someone who might even answer your call. Vanity,
Vanity, but you stretch taut the white grains in lines across the glass.
There is no question of who will take the bigger one because it's just
    you.
You wonder at the nine guitars and two basses in the room. You
    indeed
Are denied a venue — what they call an outlet for your contended
    talent.

But for now, it's you and the snake. You are walled in good and the
People stare in fascination as all six inches of your hairless flesh lunge
While the snake recoils and flashes out in riposte like a high-hat,
Trying to syncopate you on an off-beat. But your teeth sink into meat.
You shatter the snake's dream of finding the queen. You rip a straight
Long, meaty bone till it goes limp. Now that you have performed the
    wholly
Unexpected killing, you leave the lump of blood and scales to putrefy.

Your only thought is of those who walled you in alone, to face your
    mole rat
Destiny and save their ass. You nudge a clod out, then another,
Only to find more tunnels, more blocks, like a sandhog's maze.
You were liked, but not well liked. And no one thought you ever had
    a chance.

ANOTHER OPAQUE OUT TRIP

Yes. I stand on top of the ladder. No. I don't
Think I have my act together, but I am on my way.
I need to put the stuff on the stairs to melt the snow and ice.
Don't get me wrong. I'm not saying we're a couple, just friends.
But when I see you folded in prayer, I like to listen —
Not that I count. I'm just a random eavesdropper

Who is forbidden from letting on.
But I need to put it all down somewhere because of the weight.
Chosen but not called the way you like to joke.
The gallows humor of a father seldom home scarred you,
& when the first rain drops fell in the bucket
We thought the picture crossing the road was a gag

God guided us into all this suave as hell.
And I was chewing gum while the cameras were popping,
And everyone was gathered around your building —
You, a secular saint in your afterlife, hell, just don't kill
The messenger because there's too few of us left who have all our
Lousy, glistening faculties intact.

MARY MORRISON

I saw the bright type they drew collapse. My woman was in my lap.
We were caught up in some talk, & she wanted me to tap something
    back
Out of the icy white corner I had set us in. You and I have no
    right —

Dancing on a night like this — to view the pictures of where we were
At evening, planting the seed money in a start up dream florist where
    a certain
Agent Cancer has been plotting for us that we would pull through

These madcap tremorous times. Quit picking at that. I keep telling
    you. Our voices
Aren't aimed to really hurt in the sting sense, just melt away the day
Like a Placidyl pinpricked in juice. And knock off the strip bar on
    Hudson, I say

To myself. It's mischief for the youth in their brilliant clans to puzzle
    out,
And parrot, parrot, we all get lost in this frazzling, finding our magic
    numbers
Preening, graffiti the Major has patched in our dream catcher web to
    post on a site.

Roger that, my brother. Roger, Roger that. O don't go back into
    sticky
Gasoline splash downs. If it weren't such a constant hangnail flown
    off to the Hague.
The dude's a freak: last night he was licking grenadine off your
    foot —

I know, yes, he was just playing — but for real. I think it's sublimated
    perversion.
And his aunt's an old navigator for the ship they flew to get them
    from here to there.
I'd like to kick these white walls in, Lass, if only they'd stay still.

THROWING THE THING IN REVERSE

The celebrant will now approach the font. It's sprinkling out & we
    all concede
That we will with God's help. After that, it's tea and Italian ices.
    The kids are playing
Games again in the garden, & what the weather will do
Next is the source of some come contention after last night's black
    out bender.

But the program teaches me how to handle situations that used to
    baffle me —
Comely women in sparse clusters passing round the name they take
    from our tags.
I go sidelong between the remnants of my friends & family, lest I am
    called out,
Give cause to halt and account for all of His good works in the midst
    of the wreckage.

They single out and sing the hymns. The pipes are sweet. People
    come distances.
They smile and cup their mouths as word goes round. Ebullience is
    coming over us.
The look of love turns crooked pictures plumb again. Today the
    angles —
The bends of ever flowing grace are surfacing from whence comes

The comforter, the peace that pauses over someone way in the back.
& the twins play tag out along the realm of possibilities where maybe
    both
Will win the cosmic lottery of spheres that falls into the late morning
    sunlight.
When one wins, the other serves us best, & on the blue and red
    stained floor

Of stone they pull pranks switching in for the other. You can tell them
Apart only by the marks on their hands, even their father gets the rascals
Mixed up. If it weren't for the fruits, it would be a lost cause side-by-side in orbit
Skipping through the fair, owing nothing, with everything to lose.

DUNCE YEARS

I fixed the supervisor in a position hard to get out of.
Don't get me wrong. I don't mean to be bragging about it.
    It was an act
Born of petty fear and low conscience. But at the time,
Living how I did squashing roaches with a slap of my shoe sole,
It seemed a karmic, cosmic violation had occurred,
And I could rectify the wrong done with a flourish over the
    keyboard.

So I draped the room in the mortician's velvet that would cover
The little leak I made to the organization — existing in pulse points,
Hollow-points, laws, ordinances, bricks and mortar, blood and badges
Starring the officers of my and foreign nations. Hell, it was a goof.
The drives where that stuff is kept don't just cough up info.
You have to coax them, make them laugh, work the finger code
    correctly.

But I admit I did wrong, even if was for the good of the community.
Jeremy Bentham's my buddy through this — through the thick and
    thin.
I praised him to high heaven when the mayor of this our fair city
Decreed cigarette smokers should have their favored smoking fingers
Removed and molded into a public monument commemorating
    Victory
Over all the little puffs and drags that plume and foul the public
    streets.

Still, nothing eats at me long. Tall red and yellow drinks in frosted
    glasses,
And me in my black shirt and just washed jeans. You get it. It's chill.
My new friend, whose name is lost a moment — a ping-pong ball in
    the lottery

Machine tumbling off in the garden, is stunning, & that's the thing about me
She likes. I'm not always stating the obvious. And I'm good on cash,
So I don't have to leave her even a second alone to go to the machine.

FRESHMAN RUSH

We gathered it in more than up.
We gathered it into a fist of teeth
Upon which they had hung a dumb
Red beet to help with the hunt
With its one good eye.

The seniors had stretched the hazing
Till half of us dropped out.
The room of slats was peacefully
Caught between breaths.
The PA was dying,
Running propaganda between smiling gaps

In the teeth of the picture that held out its hands,
Graffitied more than fair.
North equals North. One of the us
Filled in that one right. But the southern sun
Amped up everything
Till the last dost burst, leaving nothing

Not even this.

KANDINSKY IN LOVE

So anyway, it was while I was enjoying a morning drink
That the indigo bunting flew or rather curbed it on the feeder —
Blue it was and blue it will remain wither it shall go.
I'd watered it down a bit, the scotch, and had to have things
Still to mention for the people who think this has something
To do with common things, or anything at all.

It is a thing existing among other things — that's the scoop.
It does not aim at being representational. Its only referee is
Itself and maybe an old wrecked train and tore up tracks
A Northern general sought fit to scorch the peach trees with.
But here in Brooklyn we have a zoo and botanical garden
And mothers of sensuality strolling sleepy toddlers.

The bards who go to the visiting circus tuck in tight away,
Enduring this spectacle while waiting for the special bang at the end.
The honey gets rubbed out on the trail, thinking of the indigo
     bunting
And girlfriends tacky enough to break up by texting.
This blue verse is immersed in the clear serum she used to use
To make her black hair give off a radiant sheen. See,

There is both a love interest and a dizzying tango. Someone once
Dug up a buried model to retrieve the poems he had buried with her.
And you, my deepest like, my spinning prop — how could you
Sneak out into the rays and bronze without your black parasol?
You have seen the baboons in the zoo, gone to the gardens,
The library, the museum, and walked the hell out of this portrait.

DRIVING OUT OF A DRY COUNTY

How much I still wish you were here to help
This dream go smoother, to help wipe off with a rag
All the bad things that went down.
You are right. I respond best to cognitive behavioral
Therapy. But other schools have something to offer,
And all I did was turn it on automatic and spray.
No idea of getting a medal — no, no nothing.
The cleaning lady had already come.

Intelligence can run away, but
When it comes to saving the life of a brother,
Thinking itself is my enemy, and when you were lifted out
I felt the words you could not say.

And the post trauma leaves me vacant,
Just a transcendental Jones Very ambulating around the room,
Which some call heaven swept bare of agency itself.
You know I'm a bad liar.
Truth is I wonder who has possession
Of these fingers as they jitter over the keyboard,
Waiting for her to fall into my life I don't know why.
Truth is in the How You Been? as my heart's bartender
Pops the top with the bar key,
And the fair lady sets things up with something sweet and dark
From the hell of her reaching
Out to me in her Scottish hair
For something to drown out these conversations
That prattle on forever down below the well,
You know, just between us.

CONSOLATION AND LOVING OTHERS

Do you long for the constant sun?
Have trouble with applications and keeping toned?
My thing is never having the proper batteries around the house
When your gifts require them to make them run.
See? We have troubles in common, thugs and thoroughfares
Where the hoods go singly or in clusters.
I like the ones who just stay there on the street
And not the ones who give chase into my dreams of you —
The fire breathers in front of the station.

Ok. You like the island accents.
That itself I can deal with, but when they don't come through
It's like an acrostic that only you seem to see.
And youth means so much to me — the way it flows away,
Twisting and shouting till it's so far underground —

Flower children and forensic experts,
Defiant gator fans, whoever — all go under the hill.

And other beautiful things
Forever and ever to cross the bar
Where the murmurs come out of unseen sectors of the sky.

BEFORE DRIFTING OFF

I don't think this one is ripe yet. Like wineberries in the clearing,
It rings a lurid taint, bitter to the tongue, hard — not ready for
    harvest
When they brim over red plastic pails. I have been concerned of late
That I have not kept up with technology, that my processor is a robin
That hops three steps and cocks its head to listen for worms.
    Everyone else

Seems a red hawk swapping bootlegged software and knowing how
To keep funky viruses from swamping their systems. A subject, yes,
It would be nice to have a subject, but a purpose is the thing —

Like the waves of synchronized green lights that, if you hit them
    right,
Just right, let you flow down the hill to The Bottom unimpeded, like
    you
Are in Venice, either or, and are cutting the surf all in beauty or the
    other
Where the black gondolas ripple your fate while your life crumbles
    around you.
Youth just is, it happens — green like a melon or the 'cush' on
    Cortelyou Road

My stoner friends call the 'kind bud' they get from the corner boys.
Does mentioning this mean I won't get into the more conservative
    journals?

But life — it's like jumping aboard a little, marble swirled dingy and
    trying
To make it to the middle seat while the brackish water is waving
    moonlit flags —
Omens to you with all the sunken galleons gathered in the
    vertiginous cove.

And there are stories the guide tells you and your future ex, and she
Turns around winningly to imply the sharks curving in from the bay
    to find
A place to breed will have no purchase with their rows of teeth after
The flower girl sprayed stray Heaven in her wake. Here's the news,
    Hon,

Our love was devoured in spats. We, the ones who had found
The fat wineberries bitter to the tongue. And then — I still can't
    trace how —
Everything went polarized before our eyes. And it was hard to tell
What belonged to whom as we bickered through a swath of rye.

MR. GOMER, OR ALL THE PRETTY RED FLAGS

Your usual way of going about keeping things in check
Was to keep the reins a little slack. Now you've chucked
Them completely. I would guess some might condemn this leak
My business partner showed me. We, my partner and I, had our
    proposals

Filched by men on mothballs. In return, I will manipulate sleep
    patterns
So I can schlep into the unconscious the secrets of those sunshine
    raptors
Deep under a hen house where never a chicken will roost. This plan
    is actionable.

Got it. Get it. Get out. But such false cadences make the music
    brighter —
Hold down the ostinato of such words we don't look up, though
The brave drop like death from above and are ciphered in slang
    salutes.

Lord God Above, it's plain to see this sublimation, but the real ratios
Aren't so funny. I used to call it pretend, at least to myself —
But I left a gray trace on the white glove as I lowered him down
Into a hero's earthen resting place. To my surprise, live rounds
Had been subbed in for the blanks.

SECRET VALVES, STRONG RIVER

Expectations lead to disappointments. This was the gist of what you
     said
As you crossed your pale legs in the taxi that had touched down in a
     puff
Of unidentified gray dust like a cosmic milk truck that saw us
     stranded
On the corner of Hudson and 10th. Dear God, thank you for your
     tender mercies,
Your chips and salsa, the positively right looking girl, and the green
     tablets
That keep my pinball machine from tilting or going loony tunes in
     the rescue squad.

And unto you I turn my service to keep me from royally pissing off
The peaches people and suffering an epiphany in a sedan trunk or
     the dreamless
Bottom of the East River. I only answered phones for them and
     dished
Out who was who in this week's book of life name chart. I did it all.
     I knew every
Last one of them, but, anon, we turned bubbly evanescent at the
     cherry blossoms.
Alas, my soul mirror was a blank, and the living tongue of the Tree of
     Life

Spat me out, a black-jack to the head, third-degree premature keter
     burns —
"Wrong place, wrong time," lowed a travelling carnival show's two-
     headed cow.
And perched now typing on this word processing program, I am
     displacing
And sublimating the you who once rolled with me across the
     Oriental rug.

I dodge away your blemishes and burn shadows beneath your eyes.
You are the archangel in the lineup surrounded by a victim's bright,
    tattered clothes.

The government gave me the walk through — as if on a grey, long,
    warped pier.
No matter how much they made you turn left and right I never
    fingered you.
I learned never to seek the source of my Lord, lest I end up a
    victim —
The sword aflame lopping my melon, instrument of brilliance I could
    not riposte.
You, my spiritual. You, my decoder at the bottom of the box,
Pray you put in the good word for me as the roller coaster climbs
    toward

What is held in the light by friends but is mocked by men in
    nuthuggers diving
Off the deep end as you fold your hands in your lap and take the
    liberty of giving
The driver directions to let me out a dozen galaxies from your secret
    destination.
Whew! I note his name and number the way I always do in my little
    pad, thinking
If I could just come up with the right words and algorithms, my clue-
    less heart
Might throw one last horseshoe and ring the stake of this my tepid
    passion.

PLAYING WITH PILLS

My son would carry the scar for life if I tossed the spotted cow.
That's just being afraid & prudent — not finishing the sentence as
    I meant it.
All the little rainbows have caved in. And there's a cauldron

Full of brown money that is the currency of where I'd die to go.
She was too much into herself. Thought was her terse pair of black
    hose,

But why not confess that my computer has been on the blink
And under its strict governance things keep coming out sideways.
There are bones and then there are bones. Thin clear tendrils of
    spittle connecting

Me to my pretty neighbor, an infamous woman. It's hard
When all the theaters have been shut down to put yourself to taking
    task.

And what's that tingling? Why is all this so bitter sweet?
And that conference man asking if we could write like anyone —
The greatest writer in the world — would we so purloin his (or her)

Voice, or go to the skating rink where we broke our leg meaning
We're not the second coming of a poet's poet. Personally, I dig
    Kilroy.
He's everywhere, and when I was a boy everything was right.

JAMES NAYLER'S TONGUE BORE THROUGH

And the rain was gathered, soaking the thin lasers that shorn the
    knee-
Highed grass the sheep gnawed where I was lost in an English field.
Ever looked at a goat's eyes close up. They are another state of
    matter —
The plasma as the heart beats, the cup at the center of a bat's heart.
And into the witnesses, the professors of the dying fate of faith,
I jig a worm along the pond's bottom, just to see if anyone's left, any
Master of Machines who can make the combine turn the field over.

Ever try to give a three-year-old boy a bath in a sink? There's
    adamantine
Resistance of the small, super human arms as you try to turn him out
    of his shirt,
The cry that cuts like a filleting knife, the monster squeals you would
    quell
So the neighbor's above your former wife's digs won't think you're
    doing
Cruel, unfatherly things to this booger that is the one thing on earth
That keeps you doing the same old day to day when you'd otherwise
    be ashes.

It wasn't me who called them to, I have only this prognosis of
    leaves —
Heart-shaped trees from the grounds they let me out into if I've been
    good.
They beckoned me of their accord, & the donkey was pretty much a
    prop.
The judge, who is as to leaven to the congregation, called me forth to
    speak.
I pledged myself true that I had lived on nothing save blackberries,
Running along the hedge to the carnival, and it is they should
    harness the shame.

AND OTHER LIVING THINGS

You set out to create a thing beautiful in its own right.
Friends didn't always understand. They are, as you discovered,
Not always big on aspirations unless it's a nine-to-five thing.
But as the saying goes art is long, not only in its lasting,
But in the duration to tap something like the word "suffering"
They drop mockingly into what is growing in your heart.

The way I see it, just being a friend away, I mean if I were you,
I'd keep at it with the sweet, frustrated intention that is totally you.
Yeah, we all know life is ...well. But though it may amount
To thriftless praise and dodgy backhanded condemnations,
It is important you try to gather up your memories and distill them
    down.
You feel pent up. Hell, so do I with this distance between us.
But there's a certain truth to the "use it or lose it" way of looking at
    things —
God, just listen to me going on like I know what the hell I'm talking
    about.

But I'm trying at least to keep the gainsayers from toppling you,
And I use these mirrors to cover my back.

And you tried to reach into tomorrow and got only a spare tire of pain
At the butchered cover of yesterday and today.

Seek out, or I would, the really simple things that still make you smile.
Despite the cloned speech, you remember how to damn well
Stick up for yourself when it gets right down to it.
You recall the frosty omens that people said were in your head.
And deep down you know it is only their petty fears
That you might keep growing taller, and their children's children
Might not be able to cut down the beautiful tree you are busy
    becoming.

NICK

Son, during this confessional, I wish I could take your hand
And turn this hourglass up and down again until we both were
Laughing in the rooms I left behind me. You are why I stay nearby
When the back door will not open, and you're the one who keeps me
Living out these stormy days.

I'm headed down Virginia and would gladly
Take you with me, but we both know that your Ba-Ba is the black
    sheep
Of the herd. And I make my fingers sing in these silly little patterns
Like pointing this and that way when we're looking at a bird.

I never meant to leave you like this wondering what had happened.
I had too many sad days with the otters in the tank.
When I talked I watched the red flags and the eyes of firemen
Light up in the night because they knew I was a fighter.

You with your faces and the way you can't say "yellow" —
You're a real good kid, and will follow your own legends,
And the lonely heroes who were victims of the plenty —
They will talk to you as the one I left behind, but you see me
On occasions and at intersections left behind, and if
A black sheep could write, I would leave this letter signed.

RED JEEP ON EDGE

Okay, so the whole lot of it is mottled with foxing — the dull, brown
    stars
Abandoned to the basement I share with the other me, the one that
    cranks
Out the phony checks of life to my line of creditors. Okay, so what
    — I am

A pair of cigarette-stained hands moving — without grace — over
    this keyboard.
One thing leads to another, but I'm good friends with some guys on
    the job.
Strange they let me in into their circle. They are tough, tight, and
    don't spill jack

When and where they drink. They are on closer terms than a college
    team
Locker room. When I prayed "Let me in," I never dreamed just who
    it would be
To open the door. I'm basically a rocker with interest in national
    security.

Say hey, how did Marlowe go down, or Raleigh — the ones an old
    friend
Called the Spy Poets. Every laughing cadet was onto the schedule
    well enough
To buy Poe's book of poems at West Point when he was drummed
    out.

Yes, do, please correct me. And there's Pound — a true traitor — but
    not,
By any measure capable of the type of cryptology they caged him for.
I simply live and learn. Mostly fail to learn. I'm talking regular
    gender

Essentialism now. Women I mean I fail to learn about. I honestly
    can't figure
Them out. It is a Problem of Different Minds, which takes us back
    to Philomath.
Ludwig had it right, and Watts, sit on a boulder and drink and drink,
    and drink.

I know some sad endings, but that of the little middle-aged family
    tag team
Seems the saddest. But who am I to talk and prattle on. Tried that
    and failed.
Hey, Captain, here's a wad of singles for you to tuck in.

ANGELS AND SNUFF

If only the mystery of the suds borne to the shore was so pure
As that of foam down by the wharf. Do you remember then —
Or it was just a blot locked into my head dreams — how the crabs
    rattled
Sideways in their brackish cages in the blue phosphorescent tinge

That seemed to connect your vision of whatever it was to mine.
I would leave out the "seemed" except I know you like to qualify
Your logic. Truth is: you can be a real sticker for knowledge and
    belief.
And we alerted each the other about presumption and the gall of
    presuming

Some sway of just where we were going to later, after the party,
And we went of separate ways — one by one, tired, kinked in the
    knees.
But I'm not playing Cotton Mather to gather a gang.
You prefer good guacamole and salsa on a plate of melted nachos.

Look. I never was able to say what you meant to me, that behind
My laughter and shyness was basically an investigator seeking to
    uncover
You naked, which tore me up thinking about it all, knowing
That it was my astral job to stop you, to take you before you made a
    sound.

SONG OF THE SANDS

A fair shake to hold your end of the bargain up,
It would, you say, never have come to this.
Their eyes did not behold the you
You knew their dull courage might have, the tickertape
Underpinning, and the colored streamers and the steamers —
All went under, all went under in the storm.

Far off islands in gauze galaxies, your pulse went undiscovered,
Sucked up only by a dish-shaped bowl on the green tip of St. Croix.
And if an officer is laughing, hold your breath and just count
    backwards —

Because end-to-to end you lay your love.
The device contrived for your pleasure and protection.
You shuck the tasseled ears we need to keep us grounded
When the ruins will be greening over. You just laugh slower 'cause
Your secret's safe with me
And with one or two good friends you haven't met.

ALL WE DIG UP

And into this without a hope we go.
Everything falls. Everything fails. A red ribbon
Stripes the house in her dream.
The bridegroom turns out to be a louse.
Pain we swallow, under the spot where
The ribs ordain how much we can hold.

Molded, fashioned, grown from birth
Into the can we kicked down the road
Along the tracks weeds that grew like wicked twins —
Spinning in the twisted cords we gave
Issue to the woman's red twine
Fashioned sign in the windowpane.

We storms know how to strike
When unexpected by the truest flag.
The flag the red ribbon failure said
Would be the room we'd inhabit.
Level headed some must be somewhere
Else it all goes by without the twitch
Of the bride, pricking her finger.

THAT PLANE IS HARDLY MOVING, IF AT ALL

I don't know why they said I am "associated" with the agency.
It's not like some Joe running around to open auditions with my
 headshot
And list of off-off Broadway credits. And you, what are you doing
 marking
Me the listing way you do? We together are a little less than a team.

If there wasn't always someone forever involved in this contrivance —
Some attendant shucking out a moist hand towel when I'm busy
Hitting the head, or some strawberry blonde ushering in a new
 configuration
Of the mating patterns you helped me to firmly establish when I was
 high
Above the Water Club on the North 19 Ward, looking down at the
 torsos

And other parts trucks were wheeling in to load like meat onto semi
 after
Blue tarp-covered semi. No. I didn't think it was much fun either.

And why were we even then there? The Seal who high fived me in
 the corridor
Was afraid after I had told him of the jets and nature of the village
 carnival,
Because it all actually went down. I think he was from Texas, or
 somewhere
On the border — excellent Spanish, oddly seeming to be at odds
 with me.

But that was when I wasn't initially prone to opening my big mouth.
What was his name? Anthony, the janitor — he got me talking the
 game again.

And all the fluorescent lights everywhere, when infrared would be
more
In keeping in line with the level and clearances required to get at
this —

This thing borne of the Dog Star, these things keep quiet most of the
time
Except when you, me, it — I hardly know how to even address
anything these days.
My pronouns have all gone to hell.
But here and now there is hot water in the pipes,
And the water fountains are no longer signifiers of a little job I'm still
working.

SAYS MR. RICHARDS

I'm sorry but I can't
Have such expense in my ledger,
When taking you to dinner
Never leads any further than laughs
And conversation on the wraparound
Of your sofa, and I'm thinking
Maybe this friendship thing is the wrong way to go.

But all of it —
I mean the total of your crying
And your laughter
Makes it hard to come to a decision
Of where this thing is headed,
And I can live a little longer
Because we've known each other
And you mean something to me.
I find it hard to tell you.

And you come complete
With a mole a little lower than the edge
Of the corner of your left nether lip,
And your beauty is abundant,
But runs off like a shadow,
And I need time to think on you, to abandon
These strains of this romantic
And check off the secret prodigal box
That speaks Russian to my need.

THE SETTLEMENT

Even now, whatever happened escapes your grasp.
A move from here to there and the sweet, unearned love of your life
Was overboard in a underwater cave. It was an erring.
Somebody couldn't account for an earring, and the diesel engine
Of petty quarrels eddied in the river's heart until love pinned
Its sweet Sunday stab into other effigies, some currency demanded.

No. No. No. You're right. It doesn't make a lick of sense.
Hell — that's just the way it rolls sometimes.
Take care of yourself, you said. But you yourself whited out before
The sounds you thought you were making left into the air.
Despair you named your mountain. Ouija you called your game.
Slide one that here and you will next have your lover's name.
Whoever tilted this machine, friend, had forgiveness on his mind.

DEEMING WHERE YOU ARE

The times I go there sometimes I can stay on Saturn
Far too long, and now I'm there for good. My boss wants
A piece of me. And I try to follow directions to building
A bookshelf I could leave empty. Follow me down
Would be the keening of the hollow refrain. And though I can't
Mention you by name for legal reasons, and because I wear
Your ringing, sweet voice of youth in my ears doesn't mean
"Jack" has anything on you or me. But I'm talking around the point.

Bruise his head, says the traveler. Offer her chocolates for the
    holidays.
My mouth is always open like this — agape and clucking
Like a chicken in a whitewashed henhouse. And yet
I can't help to try to count your last lashes in the terminal freedom
After you leave a message on my phone. I have been where
We were weeks, damaged years later to try to find your teeth.

And the screen wavers if I drop enough.
I'm sorry to have to come to you like this, sorta shabby
Of me, but there are still the boxes of your move to deal with —
And bootless cries, yet we go on neither even saying so much
As hello, and no it's not always pretty for you and me.

And the problems of Presumption canonize our increase.
All our fault, Heaven to wherever we shall abide.

TROUBLED INSIGHTS

Long nights came on us unawares.
We wanted to play without trouble, as troubadours
Of nothing in particular, save

Our own sense of well-being.
And it was awesome for such a dwelling place
To be already created for us

To drop in on.
Mother and father, you knew
More than the lonely smoke this night lets on.

MANIFESTO OSTINATO

First, out of gloomy night, came the pink tendrils of morning.
You were making "Y" shaped things out of cups and quarters.
It was another pit stop you were inducted into by the loafing steps
Above your new place in the natural order of things. You know,
    but don't
Dare talk, about those days of being away from everyone, those days

Of spittle and obedience. No one but those who are even capable
Of taking up a bed and walking would have any clue where we go on
Into the deepest pockets of white snow, the secret recesses when
    everyone

Was let out to play, but we had to stay behind to talk to teacher —
The giver of the early antidotes and layers down of the rules of
    evidence.

You are special, but not unique in the strict sense, singular is the word
I'm hunting for, in the way you travel without any hitch to cotter pin,
Without sign to the others that you have left the chair, or risen
    quietly to roll
Back the waves of whatever voice you happen to be engaged with, or
    to —
We are still fuzzy on that point. But you are smart. You know when

And where to go or stay, what color flower will chase off
Whatever you need be rid of, how to lay a strand of hair across your
    pillow.

Just try to keep up with getting to the chemist's on time.
I find following the regimen, and not thinking back to folks unless

The words issue only from their mouth help some. The one you want
Will always be just overhead. In the crucial crises that come back
    to us,

The dusky traumas, all the sly strategies you now see before you
Are charted like a map, and only you came to decipher the legend.

REALITY CHECK

You wanted to make it short and to the point,
But you called me not only man child idiot, but also a spigot
That ran hot or cold depending on your changing trust fund.
You were always talking about the huntress
And the bounders you mistook for deer in the twilight
Of my legal handicaps. I hate to drip on and on like this,
Just when you are falling asleep, when you're too spent
From being with him, and half of you wants to get up
And give the faucet a angry twist — like when we were
Climbing that little mountain upstate, and you got a pebble
In your boot that didn't quite annoy you enough
To go to the trouble to take the shoe off and shake the stone out.
And that makes me think how you were rushing,
Always rushing, rushing, rushing to get to the top
Just so you could say you had been there and be done
With it. You actually would stare at the second hand
Of your watch, pointedly, and sigh away
What could well have been an enduring and beautiful life
Together, just because I wanted some snapshots with my
"Stupid Camera." I have never been one who cares all that much
About the subject being in focus, and now apart
In the orange light of this archaic darkroom, I look
At your long face in the fixing tray and see the glare
In your eyes go dark, like a sentence that was finished
Before it was ever written.

THROWBACK RECOGNITION SCENE

Father, further out I dare not fathom —
The sink was forever running over its allotted boundaries,
And I was hearing talk below me, and all
Of my defenses came to nothing.
I said creatures of sand were coming,
But you laughed it off in the front seat. Now,
I can't breathe so well at all those years of your corrections.
The sad predictions, all the readings — the prognosis
Of my kind was sheer rooftop lassitudes.

But I jump still the coach's hurdles, watch the crying
Water tower where I thump down in the nest of pine tags,
To dive into a diagnosis, and to satisfy the debt
You owed me the visits plummet down not
Far from the tree, and sundry sayings,
The white-hot clichés of God, or something like that.

PINOT NOIRE

You like this weather fine, with the flakes falling
From my dinner wallet, and my card even went through.
Your friends were nice talking, and I was all cap and bells.
But with each mouthful I wondered what and who in me of
Me or whomever she likes to drain is drowsing. The whole thing,
Quick kisses, and your making me into a daisy you could peel
The wings off of to drown in your eyes.

I thought the cook would always be there —
That the lobster would always crawl back to the sea.

You claim to see something in me when, what do you know,
In my own shaving mirror there is never even a face,
And you are firm, mothering whom you see as a fool lost
In this snow's silent fanfare where you could love anyone.

WHY MUST IT BE THIS WAY

This is what it amounts to, a tongue tied cherry stem
Plucked from the mouth of a co-ed, if that term is still
In use. I asked if you could conjure a hangman's knot
So I could go to the attic and get a head start on things.

Demure, you were, way out of my range — A lemon bulls eye
Who wanted a higher grade and would drink nothing
Save red wine. I'm going out on a limb with this now, but
I drew from my black quiver a three fletched arrow, and shot

Into a excelsior bale dead on for practice on the range.
I tried to study you, but in vain. You were moving so fast, so numb,
And taken with things very bizarre to like me for.
Hell, far as I can make out I'm just your average Joe.

So you wanted to try the yew tree long bow, my prize,
And clenched your teeth like Telemachus as you drew the thing
Only an inch because it was very stiff. Then, by hap, you
Another drew, anonymously, to hit the king dead in the eye.

LIGHTED AND LAUGHING

Over all the racket of the children, it really didn't matter.
I had confessed regarding the tablets I take. Maybe the host
Seated me there by decree. Maybe it was just a lovely jab —
The crazy boy cracked up, uniting him with his shadow.
And it was done live. The network advertised it would be done
Without a net. And you threw in a breezy state of grace

To get us majorly lost in the "I gave it my best shot" syndrome.
O constellation of comely brown moles on your right arm,
The proximity of my scar to your star was dripping through the sieve
At different speeds between moping dwarfs, sublimating
Slowly, but dead on accurately, unlike the imperfect mark
The man or woman inked on your bare shoulder blade.

I didn't cry. The babble didn't shatter me. It had just poked
Me with a lacquered nail as if it was all in fun. You had to make
Another dating mistake to cancel out the first one.
It was purely an exercise in an astral double negative, no?
With me on the crazy birthday boy's side, well, whose to say?
The shards might be mended, and he be made whole again.

LAST CLEAR CHANCE

Back in the shadow of the mountain, or 'rising' as they call the
    foothills
In those parts, you were a fly that swam down the open spout of a
    bottle
Of whiskey someone had set out to trap you. In other words, you
    took
The bait and it caused friction between you and your family. I don't
    know

How to say it otherwise, if I am to be candid. I am too busy snaking
    out
Of inverted syntax and the idea of the image. Both of us attach
Unusual significance to the word 'glass' as far as fatal wounds go. But

Before I rant and rat out the culprits (you know who you are), I'll
    admit
That when I brushed this morning I spat blood, just a little in the
    cold,
White, durable basin that will probably be here longer than I will be.

But I seem to be getting off my subjects — family estrangement,
    poetic games,
And murmuring flakes who open fire on themselves or others or ask
The subcontractors to make sure to build the beams high enough
    that

They can take others, innocents, along with them while they ride
Things out alone in New Hampshire. Too many movie screens to
    deal with.
"Stay away from the occult" my astrologer told me because I was
    born, she said,

Overly adept at this sort of bunkum.

PART TWO

MOON APPLES

Turning back now around the time curb. You are where you are —
     presto!
And the rabbit died when you were sixteen, passing crying notes for
     fear someone
Could intercept your texting.   Everyone was down with chest fever
     and the spangles.
The flag blushed at the mere overhearing of your conversation with
     the motley,
Medley mooded spirit of the universe when the bathwater went red.

Me? I was only an isomer, a fishing effigy clutching a boa constrictor
     you had
Given me as a cane fly rod. Now look, you'd say, that circle over there
     was a fish.
I lay her out smooth over the clear glass. And suddenly it was you,
     anon.
You spread my life open like child's putty on a comic. I was with
     someone else.
No — was someone else, and you were Gabriel's lily shining on the
     water.

After that, it was all cheese fries and shakes. We watched each other,
     cuddled,
Went down to Film Forum for Japanese films with subtitles. And
     then to Washington Square to score a taste of how it was popping
     the blue battalions
Of NYU students to give them back their New Historicist first date
     text guides,
And so on, and all the lonely shattered spectacles rattled softly home
     to tryst.

A TOAST FOR ALL MY DEAR ONES

You woke up in the smoking room where the walls
Were all on fire, and you lay there blank and empty
Praying at the sky. Everything forever —
Even breathing had become a chore, a drag upon

A cigarette that you had dozed off on. Once more,
At least, the team of volunteers —
Family and friends — who knew you, knew you
Were only looking through the walls again for kicks.

You would gladly die again, once more, save you knew
Emergency's demands of getting up and out,
And stepping lightly over the carpet's purple chords,
You touched the glass doorknob that opened to the stars

DRAWING ALONE FROM A COMMON SPRING

—For Anne

The paid price for a durable good which screws up your ledger,
As first love is prone to do, is by far worth the weird apparitions
In the amortization schedule.
Others because you ducked out, shunning my moves
At the apartment in your lycra gym stuff at the college where we
    smoked and where you shattered

A blue and white castle by my bed, have been friends of mine. But
    you have been the frame and fabric the others just colored on.
I just got woke up by another
Dream with you — my first since my divorce, and sorry my spacing is
    all off. I even hanged for you and took these notes because
Living in this illegal basement apartment the pipes are low and
    invite.
But seriously,
In high school I never knew you would track me through the peaks
    and troughs,

Regardless of who was at my side, woman or wife. And now I'm just
Kinda here, getting by, in a room where I cannot play guitar
Or go to the Virginia Museum of charity missions with your old
    boyfriend
After I left the hospital and was being
R-E-I-N-T-E-G-R-A-T-E-D into Society, crazed reprobate I was —
Despite the sudden returns of my faculties. My heart, where you
    lodge, still tosses you back to me rare nights,
When the dream catcher's net fails.

I should have done what the cookie suggested at that Asian
    restaurant we last
Dined at when you had broken things

Off (to make a point) with your fiancé. I should have brought
You down
Easy on the sofa in the basement that night. But we both know
You never make a true mistake, whatever your last name is now.

LAST LINE OF THE BLITHEDALE TRILOGY

Sharing a cig on the traumatized, unpacked boxes —
Pinch to pinch — is the most intimate act I know. I could not be
More or less than a friend. They have hazed me, & you
See it judging by your eyes & soft voice. You turn on

All the spigots that are running in the eggshell skull of my magical
    thinking.
But your birth-written, adamant smarts ask the practical questions.

Does this have anything to do with a raise in maintenance fees?
Do you think you could start with unpacking just a couple
Of your journals today & put them on the shelf?
It would be a start, & it would make her so happy to come home.

I thought I had washed a clandestine agent's love away in this life.
When you called me "a turd" it hurt.
I thought…I thought…but you think. You were
The brilliant go-getter of this murmuring & deficient heart.

THE HAT ON THE BED

Ha, brother, you really had me going when you fostered
My misplaced belief the whole thing could hold together — come
    rain,
Come shine like a stone I could crush in my fist. But the draft

Caught me unawares. I tried to seal it all tight. I tried to make
The bubble bath just right, so my son will be
Neither hot nor cold, and you could chuckle at my references.

And brother I knew whenever you stuck up for me.
I knew your word went unchallenged ever since that joker
Who tried to light you up you jacked against the lockers.

Dad was too much of a gentleman for this type of work.
You and I have engaged in it for some years. But to be honest,
I think you ought to give due diligence to the fact

That forty winters take their toll and the ones you want
Are staying in their twenties while you wonder at the gray
That lands on the barber's sheet to be swept away.

Yes. I know there's always Hamburg. There's always Amsterdam.
But think for a second. Are those the latitudes fit for an alpha
With such integrity as yours to touch down midst in a ship?

And I flash these red flags only on paper because in the beautiful
Security details they assign us to, we don't even need to hit send.
We don't talk — only to throw the ball back in enforced, serious
    silence.

THE IN'S AND OUT'S OF ADOPTION
(URIEL ANGEL SANCTIONED)

I was told by a guy who knew his shit and had access
To secure databases that he ran you. You popped up as a Deep Net
    Plant —
And please, Buddy, keep this to yourself. You have already finished
    your work —
Your telepathic melon has been split and reveals it spills when it gets
    drunk.

But, basically, so what? We're Clueless. Stick to your Drum 'n Bass
    programming,
Handle Yer Hofner, lay down lovely tracks sublime.
And if something happens to come your way, stay calm and hit
A happening club hard that night, but please don't mention this
    poem, Leakymouth.

Talk the usual bullshit; smoke a roll' up, and get down.
Yell EVERYBODY GET DOWN! NOW! GET DOWN! GET
    DOWN!
And for every one hit there are two-dozen misses. We cloud all
    notions of heroism.
I Loved the lingo we, the three of us, tossed innocently around the
    table at George's.

Me? I'm in in in it up to here, like a stuttering Sergeant knee deep in
    boots in the
Mush where an enemy's name was written on the bricks named UR.
    Strutting back
Where the beginning began — save your own digs time was back in
    Atlantis.
Sorry, Jim, she remembers past Africa, past a villainous monk
    beneath his monocle.

ALKALINE SHINE

If you plied back the hair of the black rabbit, just in a dime shaped spot,
Underneath was pink flesh. All the confessions had little eyes in
    them —

Like a cluster of tadpole eggs waiting to ripen. It's okay Sad Clown,
    these

Images are drawn from nature, but it's bad to have many tiny pores to
Get tweaked out over. It's much better to have — from my vast clinical
Experience — trysts behind the dumpster with partners whose troubles

Are more all of a piece, symbolic, if singular, when they are falling apart.
This is documented. I'm not just making shit up. Anyway, my chosen
    one

Had the keys to the green house on grounds. The floor was concrete

And staff had no clue that we could find the love we lacked on the
    outside.
It was where she worked in the day because she dug the flashing tool
    into

Her palm when she got news her father was to remarry, and she would

Not be allowed on pass to be part of the ceremony. I felt for her and we
Made love mixed with tears that night below the Wandering Jew
    hanging basket,

And the next day the team announced an out trip to King of Prussia
    mall,
And that brightened her until she later saw I had shaved my head.

FOREVER GONE

My place was yours. We shared
Household chores, who would venture
Out for coffee in the morning. Your
Stop was nearby, & that was a big plus.

This is what I can remember
Of the days before we got married.
I remember lying alone in a hammock
Caught in sudden gusts and thunder,

We were an aching set of bedsprings,
Rattling in the early hours of morning,
Taking naps after picnics
& leaving shards & sharks' teeth, here in my hand.

THE SAFETY

To be honest, as men do breathe, this tasteless wreckage is my herd.
I offer up the best I can to you, whether I be a tiller of the ground
    or not.
But lately, I have been drawn to my guitar's sweet, steel strings.
    Although,
It's a more popular medium, I draw my pick largely unnoticed.
    The only time

The bar shuts up its collective mouth is when I end a song.
    Then vaguely
It dawns on them something, a mere lubricant, is missing and social
    friction grows.

But I drink on the house and take home a few bucks — it ain't so bad.

Heck, Campion is canonized for thumbing his jangling lute, but my
    audience
Has never heard of Campion. They would gladly see the Lyric burn,
    the singer
Get what's coming to him for parting his lips in song. To me, it is
    little wonder
That the plucker and poet, David of the Psalms, was a good assassin.

But the trees are closing in, as I stated elsewhere, and the severity
Of unbuckling belts for a good whopping is actionable. But dulcet
    ringing tones,
Binding in their counterpoint, are like intuitively tracking of the
    factors —

Trajectory, wind speed, and target movement and plotting a way
    to get
The Hell out of location, if one is to diminish the better part
    singlehandedly

Of an enemy platoon.   But what the hell do I know. I'm a singer,
A writer of song, a poet, a maker — and the other me is that guy
   on the F train.

RECESSED BLESSINGS

They piled up the work.
They called you in and then they said this,
And you never really ran away
Like you should have.
Your getaway would be to go
To some farther safe haven like the school
Where the knocks were softer
Than a homebound proverb's hands.
The throwback driver of the school bus
Was your only true confessor,
And when he got the secret out,
The next day he pinned a lovely badge on you
Of pink construction paper with your name
In glue and blue sparkles.
And it's funny how you will throw
Your tricks only under pressure.
And the others all admired you,
Huddled on their green seats, bouncing
Harder at the back. It almost fun how it
Gives you the salt taste of this solace,
To know the tin soldiers boys were
Supposed to play with
Could rescue you all these years later,
Never to leave
One of their own behind.

A HINT OF SWEET SCIENCE

Look. You had too bad of a kink for the alpha thing.
It went to the extremes. Allow me to name them.
They are as robbers at autumn's thin evenings. (I think we both
Know mum's the word.) I don't know if they would
Use you against me or take what has passed between us
And chart your shudders into an algorithm in the traffic of the city,
And the Pineapple on the big island draped your uniform with
    medals
With your ciphered topology charting of our random goings.

But O the beaches of Patmos and the shattered souls who thereupon
    trod —
Gimme a second. I was going somewhere with this. Yes. I was
    nodding my consent
To leave metropolis because you had all those punks
Write my name on the shards they dropped smugly in the collection
    plate.
I read and run — that's my story and I'm sticking to it,
And all the little gulls and subscripts flew off into the moonlight.

RESTORATIVE YOGA ("IT'S A BEAUTIFUL LIFE")

You have slid into your new jeans a week in a row. Worn the weather
Of winter's going somewhere else and now the globe is smaller than
    before.
What could you do to renew something beautiful in this your life?
Yesterday you gathered like things and evened pictures round the room.

Maybe buy some seeds from a brown catalogue that has been so long
In the ancient attic. I don't know what else I can give you; for the
    moment I'm spent.
It's like that little death of the waves when you try to mound the sand
Into the perfect pillow beneath you're head. And the children are
    charging

To their shin bones in white, always inviting, always threatening
    froth.
But I don't want to get into the old graybeard thing. Give me
    Emily's Dog Days —
She knew how to don imagination's tulle better than a crumpled old
    hack.
But she's just a preference — like every pale woman, or honey in the
    hive.

You want the facts: I like effortless perfection in an adherence
    contract.
I like fishing largemouth, out in the pads — knowing enough from
    old men
To let them play with the thing, think they can succor their deepest
    hunger
Before you, he, she, (never they) grab hold and sets the hook deeper,
    harder.

NEGLIGENT DESIGN

It had become for me
As to a dying thing – this naming
Of women had a hollow something.
It was a dream of God going blind
Yet seething.

Still, it could happen
In these days of rain and ceremonies
And such exceptional rewards,
And of the clouds and of the sea.

THE RUSHES

You're right. The day flows better when your mood is colorless, when
You creak across the iceberg of her blue irises and don't fall into some
    great
Freak of bloodshot what-did-we-do-last-night? type of pale horse
    regret.

My son has been possessed of greater scope of late. And I am
    extremely joyous
To hear how he is piecing the breakup, at last, together better —
Like the seals in the zoo, for long they kept swimming through the
    jig-saw.

And now they are being good seals he can piece together, having, as
    he has
Gradually taken in, that his Baba is going to be only a visitor.
    A loving one,
But one…wait…this is making me say, and I was to remain colorless
    in mood.

That's the challenge when you just let yourself go like this.
    A contract drawn
One minute can be broken the next. The four corners of the walnut
    box I tap out
Sometimes have issues crawl out of them, which were subsequent in
    nature.

Heck, blood always rises to its own level. This thinning of memories
    is natural.
I'm really tired of the forest and the trees when the wood is slowly
    starting
To break off into single limbs and crawl like fire ants toward the
    castle.

BYRON ON THE BEACH

In the sleepy longings that hover around you as you are sprawled,
The last heir to your throng is duly numbered. You whiten in your
    moon age
And the sheets leave their sleep scars on the inside of your wrist.
Some coffee would be nice, & in this your blonde yoga time, I succumb
To the sleepies in your eyes and agree to go to the bodega for some
    joe.

You know you can't change me, & and I know I can't change you.
We don't care much — each serving the needs of being the other's
    other.
After all, we're adults here. You are not my central nodal domestic
    angel.
That one I chose over you for my primary whom unto you at times
    may tether.
If they only got it, the fully-matriculated death-do-us part faction

Of the room then we might not be so depressed and scanning hands
For rings on the subway or bus. But we have contrived a pattern
    that works —
I did it in a hospital when I was hypomanic, that is the time most
    works
That weather time get worked out. All the elements were there.
You helped out too, behind the ice machine where the camera could
    not see.

But I'm still a show-me kinda guy. So did you prove, along with the
    other two,
That one unto one prejudice was a peculiarity of our larger culture.
You were fond of the term you coined: obverse ethnocentricity, looking
At the gemstones and coins of Caligula, and the elegance of line on
    the vases
Made in thatched shanties. The Book of Mormon was simply excess.

COME VISIT, BUT DON'T STAY

All I have to say to you is "Thank you for listening."
When at curfew, they suck the air out of the airtight room,
And they mix it with knockout gas, I try to remember
There's still a chance I won't go to State, up in Rockland.
And once I awoke cradled by Junior and some blood
I had never seen before, slinging me down on my cot.

A confessional dissertation makes you loose with your talk.
The soap that didn't sud or clean your body, which I complained
About in Team Meeting. One of the interns was impressed
I knew and could use the word 'hypnogogic' correctly.
After I, under gag order, sacrificed the sleep which lack dost murder.
I was never into the Scottish play. It's beyond the reach of tragedy.

Better to think of Alice and I under the water tower,
Peeling the pine tags out of her long hair afterward.
You came after that, my Phi Beta Kappa true love. I told
You of the days in the halfway house, and you grew sad.
And later in the room Faulkner wrote his first book
We laughed at the raffle winner with her maudlin story.

Who could have guessed the story would come true,
Or that you would be too chicken to sneak in some smokes.

TAKE OASIS

She's using that tone of voice again — quite apart
From the others, behind the bushes. I knew some day,
Some time, everyone would be given enough rope
For the purposes of a young gentleman practitioner.
And I know you don't often follow me where I opted
To be sent. The bank statements told me
The rice papers tucked under his blotter were jokers.

But the measures everyone would go to were beyond me.
No lie. Telling a kid with a bad habit you're going
To chop his head off because he dare stand up before
The king is not positive thing. But I stalled
Like a twelve-point buck on the wall and offered,
I now confess, to varnish my own head. But that
Was just a dream, and I am not a dreamer.

I heard they auctioned off the coffin, and the house
Brought in an absurd number. It takes a hell of
A village to shatter someone who is called, much more so
One who in bars the way you do call yourself a traveler —
You with no map, hope, respect or the things you were told you
Needed by the ones who whisper to the mirrors they were chosen by
While you were busy running around on fire.

JUST BEFORE LIGHTS-OUT

When it could be the dawn of the board's future decision, suddenly some yellow
Hive breaks off and we see you are sweet at heart. The rumor caught and flew

Into the pile of gathered tinder that you had used to set the blaze that made
The supervisors let everyone go free — even the archangels, even the old man
Who had lived imprisoned in the tree until someone I was once close to

Carved him out of the curly maple. I know I'm nothing special. Investigators
Come and go with the glistening points on silver shields.

I had a thing for you for a long time — a long, long time being bereft of your music,
Denied the visuals of what you were wearing, kept apart from your wet, rainy
Beads. You were the one in the station behind the station glass, where I was like

Confessing my balance was not in the system. I talked to you through a perfectly
Circular whole. And after the incident, for days I guess, your hands trembled

At the sound of each airliner. And so it goes. I've cloaked you deeply and shyly,
As if in a snowdrift — like the lucky one you return to at your shift's end.

But we don't live in a perfect world. It's enough they even come by
    each week
With the little book cart. I never quite manage to catch your
    attention,

Even through this distance. No slick page could hope to gloss you
    and your pile
Of last month's fashion mags someone, someone you'll never meet,
    left behind.

TOOK A BLUE CANOE

Fish? Certainly. Blue betas and red betas kept
In separate snifters so they won't tear each others'
Long, delicate fantails apart. And I want to provide context
For the image of you down by the old mill pond
My family sold to the Battlefield Association. And
When you were heavy with the gift we made it
In the back room of the antebellum house.

I am so glad I met you, even if I failed you in the end.
Things could have turned out differently, but then the gift
You sacrificed your life for never would have entered the world.
I was amazed at the power of your forgiveness.
I was amazed at the pictures you took time to convert to prints.
I am still piecing it all together with numb, trembling hands —

I practiced learning to forget how trees grow.
The winding access road into the Wind River Mountains
Where you, me, and my genius hiking partner all got lost
Seventy miles from civilization, I slept with a sheath knife
On my chest and nearly used in a tragic scenario.
I'm not certain I ever told you about that part.

Stunned by the glue I huffed hidden back in the day,
I wasn't even enough me to have you return my calls.
The smell of gasoline will ever be the reddest of roses.
When time came I told the truth, or my truth, with
The many years tossed like a Frisbee on a summer night
When the fireflies winked back God's warmth and buzzing wrath.

YOU'RE VERY GOOD AT WHAT YOU DO

So this is the weight that clicked all around her as she stepped through
The beads of just having to be a girl. That's hard enough — add on
The crackle of the leaf pile composed by the rake skittering over the
    drive.
Voices have a valence, a drifting frequency, like the waves that crashed
As her father waved her in from where she was slowly drifting.

How could anyone mark on the molding, just how much louder
The voices would grow, would grow with age — and the ruthless
    peak and trough
Patterns that would leave one seat empty in one freshman year
    classroom.
It was no longer a matter of containment. She had played out all her
    sly tricks.
And like most beginners who carried a overnight bag into the adult
    unit, she

Glowed like wine. The leaden veined shadows laced
The linoleum as she made a flat line for her admissions signature.
    Just one place
In body, but she carried the called out destinations from the bus home,
Only to be in this place where they called multi-colored codes
And from a brimming plastic cup gave her something yellow.

She had just dyed her hair for the first time. Her pupils pulsed little
    black pansies
In the metal mirror where an old woman was scratching her legs in
    the light.
And there was laughter, and the low notes of the xylophone that
    quelled things —
Quit the stations from flipping so quickly. She was safe from all the
    looks,
Safe from the books, like a star no one would ever discover.

MERCIES

This one is not like the others — several real men are stomping
Above the mattress, stomping in a targeted,
Menacing way so deafening I go in the other room.

I had just put my phone down. I was telling my kid not to be scared
Of the monsters under the bed, but he didn't buy into that dad jive.
    Pass
The pills if they chase away these monsters. But I know

They don't. I call a friend on the Force. He said call back in the
    morning.
I called my ex, the housing lawyer. She simply said to move.
What about the new sign outside with big red letters NO PARKING?

What about the grey sedan with black windows?
What about the white cards on the dashboard? The only ID
Visible from the outside? I'm not important enough

To hassle. I just want my mail.
It has been a week since I got my mail. They used
To throw it down the stairs every day but Sabbath.

Now I want pills that say goodnight. I want to walk
Unafraid for the juice. I want my junk mail flyers. I want it all,
    all the noise,
All the murmuring, all the slams to be a check marked paid in full.

ONE HOUR AT A TIME

From the bed where I've spent the day dreading
Each time the blurred footsteps would pass again.
Without alcohol, scary the world begins to flower
Into open buds of cruelty and what not arching over.
They must have been trained. How else would
They flush from the floor like nervous quail.
Only where is the guide, the pointing dog,
To ready me for this explosion into the inevitable?

DISHRAG

I deserve no gender.
You can have the covers.
Friends point
& I laugh at my fate.

It's my fault —
Losing it all, the seashells
Saved for a necklace,
The key to your happiness.

& this is the real me
Buried in the pillow.
The cat scratches the baby's
Face while I'm on duty.

You are right to be
Forever rid of me, &
This little axe is working its magic
Hacking off who I was in my head.

THE ONLY HANDWRITTEN ONE

A bell is not lifted easily; you showed
Me pictures of all the failed efforts.
Eventually, however, the bell that weighed a ton
Sat plumb amidst a crest of ivy,

Peonies, teakwood, and was stunning. I told Shannon,
"Yes. She is very pretty, but it's not that" —
An "all of dark and all of bright" kind of thing.
& if you see anything in me, please don't let on.

Michael says love songs are odious and reduces
People to props. But going back —
What was the thing called inside the bell?
You had a word for it I did not know.

But I nodded and un-hunned like I knew
What the word was. I did know what you meant.
But I was embarrassed not to know the word.
Was it made of silver? A bright thing in a dark place?

And I am doing my best to hold true
To my promise not to call until after the Holidays,
When we can sit and have coffee and talk,
And I can open this notebook and show this to you.

MY JOB FOR YOU TO NOTICE

Ready, if need be, to throw this one. Dad likes to work with his
    hands —
Searching colons for polyps, perforations, and other malformations.
Tell me, Dad, how it is to make a table, to slide a dove tail joint into
    place,
Now that you are taking woodworking at your (and my) old high
    school.

Sometimes I feel like that first table you turned out — wobbly,
    unsure
Of its feet. Sometimes I wish I had four legs like an ass, so
    I could wind
Down the spiral canyon trail with more grace, not braying in the
    wind
With an angel on my back, guiding me down, deeper into the pit.

Do you remember throwing the softball, at first in clumsy lobs,
Then, in youth's fog chamber, overhand in curves in the falling dusk.
On Sundays I cut the lawn with the electric mower, bagging green
Heap on green, leaving behind straight lines of pain I never grew
    out of.

FOR GRANTED

Walked home as dusk darkened
In my Orthodox neighborhood.
Lay under my sheets clothed, hiding
From the bloodshot eyes of Christ,

Dreaming of groves of sycamores
Where I could take up my bed and walk
Through the star's skid marks
Into the dawn of dreaming dogwoods,

Preferring the pealing moon
Where the orphan kneels,
Praying to see in the shadows
Its mother coming closer.

NOW AND ALWAYS WITH YOU

Why do you keep calling
When you know it makes it hard on me?

See my cortex,
Deem me weird. This texting is working my hands overtime.
If only it could be clean and simple like the pure
Syntax of a Quaker journal, or the dark emblem
Of Mary Dyer flagging from the gallows.

I cannot change
Or alter this syndrome. The red book is splayed open
Under thatch in a public house,
Open wide as the Black Sea.
The plates have learned to cut the running lines.
The charred, clicking episode of death's long log-in.
It is resisting the whim to bash the fourth wall in again,
Like an ad where a man steps out in green scrubs
Touches your forehead and says, "Count
Backward from a hundred please."

When the stuff really kicks in, and your lids are heavy as with wine
Or going under as to ether dripping,
She plucks you out, yanks you to the stage,
And saws you clean in half. Voila.

All recursive looking back is a joke, a judgment of the learned
        hand —
As life goes on without us, leaving the poem scratched,
Grainy, flecked with the last kiss.

Stale breath under the ear, musk of bread and wine —
O dark Oinos of all sex forgotten, the stiff, starched tablecloth
Spread out and scraped clean of fish and crusts.

You of the crowd wonder, allowed
To let your thoughts wander where the great mind wills —
Not your will, nor again randomly scudding the birth canal, the
	guide's
Echoing a man in a blue suit who ushers you to port,
Who ties you off, while everything in the landscape goes as maple-
	red
As a swept and garnished pile of leaves where you emerge
With a name and ID, the little sparkly commas dancing on the ward
	chart
Panning a shot in slo-mo of your first cry into the world.

You are healing slowly — whole in the flicker and dangling fantails.
Every last tattoo is telling you your work here is done.

GAG ORDER

So we have similar agendas, lack of schooling, falsified documents —
This doesn't mean we have to share a berth together.
You fetch this out of an unforeseen 'sharps' box in the station &
    presto!

I like your long standard issue coat your partner must have sent you.
But one of a perfect pair of brunettes just Johnnied me a good five
    second
Lock on, eye to eye, & summoned me into a rather quizzical duh,

In which all I could do was order the chap next to me (who is, I
    think, a Mason),
Another blended scotch & act like I was listening to the band. I got
    word
To knock off talking about the project in public, so you are all I have.

The courtship of the crossroads where my leaky prey landed himself
Was a tidy piece of work, only know I wasn't there, was home sick —
Sick on a plane listening to all his pretty songs, while the Sergeant's

Needle, out of ingenious design, kept skipping in its final groove.

PART THREE

26TH AND ATLANTIC

The officer laces his book with traces of burnt tire.
The lyre had prints on it and would have led back to the woman.
This is B-grade stuff, like late night TV when I was being raised.
Digital lacks the swimming fruit flies: I gotta give it that.

This is how I think about us. I'm looking at you through
The wrong end of a hand-held, brass telescope.
You see me as a man-child buoyed in the gray, choppy waters,
Drifting deeper into the margin each time you look up from your
    thriller.

At some point either I will be lost forever. I will drown, or
Be taken ashore by a hero lifeguard. You wiggle your big toes
In the sand cake you made to keep your feet from getting crazy red.
I sign out on the green float you rented for my lifetime.

MR. VERY

Six cops, two paramedics, some geese a-laying, faces flickering
In and out like the pink tongue of a snake,
I was in the covert of a drugstore along a Manhattan drugstore.

I had succumbed in a public elbow. Four days on my feet,
Not a dime, no ID, no keys. I waited patiently then just
Collapsed without even my shoes. I had shed them, donated

Everything to the greater good of power brokers, morticians,
Street musicians and the guy that screwed on the new beer taps.
I had never really seen a quarter: I mean really seen it. The tiny,

Shiny bit of power I gave the homeless feeling like a bigshot.
Here I was getting a taste of the street myself.
Here the ambulance. Now my balm, now my salvation.

NEIGHBORS

The feet above my head are worse than ravens.
I'm a guy needs solitude.
Gone is that mercy, gone, mincing the grace the dance possessed.
No one believes: they think I'm a head case, which
Might be true, but not as sure as the stomping I've endured.

O call the cops. File a complaint against those who keep
Me up Saturday night past midnight to reconvene on the morn.
One main guy, and on weekends his friends.
They drink beer, use their boot heels to make the floorboards bark
    and hiss.
Last night one discovered banging a skateboard. Duh.

They are as hornets lodged in mine ear — stinging, stinging.
But who can I finger? I never see faces.
I walk by them on the street daily.
And they don't speak — not loudly enough for me to hear
The voices that are singing this morning in church.

FLAGGING YOU IN

Like a blur behind a rice screen instead of your height
Reflected in the full-length mirror, you were more ballet
Than this still-life bowl of petals. Others gawked at your abundance.
In the mirror the others melted into leaves.

The one who had a thing for you — you would not let in.
You, moving so slowly, could barely catch up with the present.
The overseer was on top of it all. He made nature's course
Richer and more robust. He signed off on the transformation.

Even now a shower of fresh rain calls you up from where you lay.
Even now a shadow of the one who loved you is pierced by a voice.
Lost in the clacking branches was another self you had taken
    prisoner.
In your blind beauty, you were betrothed to a ringing bell.

CHANCE HAPPENING

They ruin our climbing higher, higher.
In the dump we were checked by the guy who thought flying
Our balsa wood planes was not an assigned usage.

And my time on this laptop,
The typing of these letters is a waste of time to the neighbors.
This is not a mirror talking. I hear them through the floorboards.

So this refers to this. But don't coin a phrase or term.
This is broken at the bottom of the box.
So much shaking and digging of hands is what broke it.

If only we left well enough alone, if only we had patience,
If to find in time what fate threw our way. We suffered our hurry
Meddling with providence, that blind and deaf provider.

THE WELCOMING

This is throwing guests in the pool —
Everything encircled with yellow hazard tape
Because a supervisor lapsed on her watch.
Now Earth at the turnkey — spinning round, presto!
Summer lingerers watch for gray arcs.

Yes, she was one significant other. Lost forever.
Shame. She came on a silver train.
I asked did you bring cigarettes?
Her new lover was a concert violinist.
She was too chicken to bring the smokes through security.

The one I still know has my ring hid somewhere.
I can't afford a lawyer to push things through.
My boy, champion of my heart, is physically
In her custody. I pick spiderman up from school
Twice a week and go to eat mac and cheese at the café.

If only the murmuring mind crowd would thin out.
I want to bathe my son forever.
I'm scared of passing on whatever I have to him.
I don't want him to suffer the visitations
Of the guests, dropping in and out, wholly uninvited.

SCENE FROM CORTELYOU

Now, to set the mood: a red van, broken graffiti,
The white bulbs hanging in the dark departing Grand Central.
We are at the mercy of grace and precision.
We, the passengers, the tired travelers, are set here to trace

What the actuaries chart out and what it does
To the city comptroller's books in between the ledger lines.
You and me constitute, for the sake of argument,
A "we." During an episode each of us can make a "we."

Now that the cards are splayed on the table, I would like to know
Just what you, beautiful gypsy, meant when you said I should
Cut down on the mind travel. I wondered what you meant —
How you could tap a whole range of frequencies at the table.

Or were you duping me: sixty-bucks forked over every session.
Two-hundred to have special candles made to deflect
The spirits you said were afflicting my dented aura.
I'm a sucker for a pretty face; my game's on fire.

COMPLAINT AND SUBTERFUGE

I play guitar through headphones.
My neighbor bangs and stamps.
The landlord said I could play through headphones.
It was an oral condition of our lease.

It's hard to write poetry at all like this.
(It's hard to write poetry any time.)
The neighbor sniffs me out, as I write. He seeks
This chair so he can creak the floorboards above me.

This is a utilitarian poem. I write
To stay in one spot and not make noise.
Even these keys might give me away.
The letters wink secrets on the screen.

For months my neighbor and his brother
Have had friends over to raise all hell
Above my bed. I breathe through my nostrils
Quietly like a horse tied to a post.

COMEDY CLUB

Drum fill please. The audience is in tears.
Hysterical laughter fills the joint.

It's hard to tell they're laughing and not crying.
That's when someone reached out to touch me,

And I knew. I had sprinkled their foreheads
With the water from the font. Infants were presented

And their crying was stilled with a few drops.
There were some hecklers, but mostly the audience

Promised to see and guide the child through life.
I had another gig uptown so I didn't dwell

On a dimple or the one who was so still
I though we would have to call an ambulance.

But the babies kept coming.
My humor was wearing thin. The procreative crowd

Seemed to be in labor right there in the pews.
Midwives were brought in and said to "breathe."

And I quietly stepped down
And made my way out to the avenue

Where no one was watching over me,
And a light gray rain was beginning to fall.

NINE IRON

A blanket alongside the links was my tryst —
The seventh hole was trembling.
I was nineteen then and stayed —
A man-child in his prime.
My sights now
Are stuck on lovely twenty-eight
I've had a few jobs.
Bookstores, racketeering, and adjunct gigs.
I can be a serious —
Liked by my students.
I teach letters to dance on a screen.
I teach dough to rise.
I don't practice writing,
But typing in the mirror too fast to follow.
The mirror is my governor.
The good angel winks and pinches my cheek.

A MAN IN A CERTAIN HOUSE

It went down when everyone was half asleep, early morning
Robe around him, grapefruit half, sitting on the stoop. His face
Was shaven clean. His feet were clean. The shot rang clean.

He had clipped too deeply a nail and drew a thin moon of blood.
His mother had died last night in a car crash, or was that
The remnant of a dream he had time to time —

In the soul fulfillment center. He promised himself he didn't
Think it. To think it, he would be a monster.
He would have been he first to hear the news.

He was playing beach music in the gray slush.
Rumors went around about his full deck
Ever since he had gotten back from the war. Nobody

Came out and said anything. The world for him was
A cracked sash watching men in camouflage.
Some kids smashed the pumpkin on his stoop.

The pills from the V.A. helped a little.
"Hey neighbor," he said when he was out of the house — his
Mother's house — scraping up October leaves.

Then came early morning we heard the shot.
No one much bothered to come up with a reason. The ice cream
Man made his usual rounds.

KNOWING, NOT KNOWING

And that's how it went. You and your other
In a staring contest when the wind tossed the willow
And it was raining out. He was a damaged man
Blowing candles on the red velvet cake. You saw
Something of your self in him. You ate of the cake, too.
He praised your beauty, and you blushed a guilty red.
His disorder created codes out of innocent welcomes,
His intuition read the words running in your head.
But you would never confirm him. Just left him guessing.
But you could talk and say when he was going to say
Before it came out of his mouth.   It was a gift he gave you.
But whose thought was whose got hard to tell. It was like
Two ventriloquists in a tangled argument.
He took you to the restaurant down where the road bends.
He ordered salmon, which is what you wanted,
And you felt the pack of playing cards in your pocketbook.
You had gone to Atlantic City without him,
And that is what his hard feelings were about.
If he knew what you did in Atlantic City, he would
Water his pillow with tears. You said you just played
The slots and didn't talk to a soul. He saw through that.
That was why he was under the willow where the light green
Tassels whipped him out of sorrow.

MINOR ALTERATIONS

They are my people. Please, let me talk to them.
They speak in tongues in in in the cafeteria of life on the Outside.
They eat the bland food fed to them to keep their nerves at bay
At dawn when they are rattled to rise and face

The cuff tightening thick around their bicep. Halfway dozing,
They crack their mouths for the thermometer.
Yes. They have had a bowel movement the day before.
Breakfast at nine. They stare at the TV or knit scarves in the
    rec. room,

Make small talk with slurry tongues and dry mouths about
    discharge dates.
The orderly rolls out the chosen, charted for a round of shock.
One receives baskets of letters each day.
The rest of my people seldom see a soul, except on Sunday

Big visitor's day. Then my people's own people
Emerge with nervous, porcelain smiles, shamefaced, needing a
    cigarette
Or an excuse to step out and walk around the grounds
Around the picnic table, smoke, and hope it's not in the blood.

BRITTLE DAYS, NERVOUS NIGHTS

These walls should be made of bees wax
And not four (or is it six?) sides,
And when the light hums through
The slanted blinds shed the inner light.
The A/C drowns out the street
Where I permit myself to walk in a stew
Into Manhattan on the F or 4/5
To meet a friend or run an errand,
But I always want to head home
To the advertised loft I rent.
My wife calls me agoraphobic,
But lately, I am growing fearless.
I have become translucent
Like the back of a honey bee.
And my wings make the sound
Only the profoundly sensitive hear,
The drones, the hungry queens.

ONLY BY PROXIMITY

Most of what I wanted to be has come to nothing. Pity.
So much with possibility, all that was wasted.
Sept. 19, another day, strummed some guitar, farted around,
Went digging in my change bucket to get

Enough to buy a forty of beer. I had told myself
I'd devote the day to Chaucer and
Try to get through another Bach minuet,
But there was change enough for two forties, so there you go.

Dave called. We're on for Friday,
But I'm not counting on anything till the tape is rolling.
In my world schedules are shifty. I'm wired and transmitting,
      even now.
Took my four lithium, etc. my shrink called a "cocktail" as he stands.

O praise the Lord for the pharmaceuticals that keep this lost soul
Tethered to more or less reality, both feet on good old terra firma, tip
      top,
Ducks in a row; that kind of stuff Salt the Earth people come up
      with — the Blessed
Who differ only in the space they occupy.

THIS STUPID DIG

I've been out here out on the summer working the same map —
The topology of tribes, beads, bribes, and brides.
It was adequate, where I went and first ran into in a class
My truest love, granddaughter of the joint head of staff

Dab in the middle of Nam. I bought her a ring of blue pearl
With a tiny little diamond set center. Even though that's all history,
If you ever see this in a conspiracy documentary, please,
You meant more than St. Charles Street to me. But she's fazed,

Another face laid in memory. Should we fronting all this to go on?
The pairings, and vintages that show rare spices had been imported.
Black labs with their wild pink tongues, the site overseer walked
Between the twine that was my love's pirouette and the laudatory

Trading fourths the band took to please the challenged visitors.
Ho. I'm getting this wrong. The dogs were when we were in an
        undisclosed
Location. I guess I'm writing to please a friend away.
Someone unlike me who prefers morse to ouija.

And pearly late October skies. Things live (and die) by schedule, at
        least
In the looking back. I have been given some gifts by friends I love.
And I have been given likewise by enemies far, I thought, in the offing.
And I fold my hand sometimes, and ask that this be good toward
        grace and providence and enough.

NYC, SIXTEEN

Her Body was ultraviolet.
Committed to memory.

She shared.
She shared —

What she had was theirs —
Gauze.

Magnets for the children.
She uttered "forever" just once.

But he disappeared
Like an eclipse on his Harley.

This was the time
She fell out with her people.

She lived in Alphabet.
She was pretty, had

Offers shaming to hear.
An apple was a blessing.

She never nodded.
Never hooked.

A man
Gave her glassine packets:

The bathrooms had cameras
The public had cameras

Saw what it did
To people slumped

Beside the vegetables.

EVERYONE'S TIRED OF YOU

We talked on the phone this morning.
You wanted my assurance that the past will
Still be here to stare back at us.

Geez. You worry yourself sick:
And over nothing, over utter nonsense.
And no, I can't say for sure the face

You see in the mirror is you.
And here's some news: you're going gray.
Pick up a clump of hair from

The barber's chair.
Word. It ain't blonde baby. But you're
Lucky to have hair at all.

And who tries to talk to the sea lions
In the zoo at Prospect Park? You thought
They were doing tricks for you alone.

I'm through hangin' for now. Don't call
Or text me. And don't come through buzzing me
To hang out in my crib.

DELIRIUM TREMENS

You, my friend away, had pizzazz — a certain I don't what or why.
The steps you took you took as if walking on the moon. You were
    admired
Like a new red fish flown in from a purple coral reef.
And who was I to assign you a gender — to say which way you go?

Who was I to give away what you dittoed in the sky that bright
    June day?
That day everyone scattered when the dolphin washed ashore
And the media crews arrived with booms and gas masks in case
It was a terrorist attack. Yes. You were tumult in the clouds,

Knowing secure information, none of which you let onto. Nobody
    knew
Whose side you were really on, though it is reported there is footage
    in a vault.
I met a man who knew you, or claimed he did, but he couldn't cough up
Any evidence that would convince the higher law or authorities.

Where you were was a secret, even to you. What trauma caused your
    disability —
Well, let's say it was an accident in a camp as you were climbing
A unmapped mountain in search of the true fountain of youth. You
    failed
As you slowly allowed for the dusty gravity that you were born to fall
    through.

WELL, WELL, WELL

I was walking along — then, Wham! I fell into this,
This — I don't know what to call it. All this funny business
That made my knee jump at first, then like caterpillar —
Or an estranged lover's eyebrow — brought patterns
Like colored cobwebs in on us as we made our way

Through this place — wherever it is I you and I are.
Whew! I knew there was no use trying to resist. I almost
Yelled "Whoa! I'm yours. You got me now!"
I swear I had none of this in mind when I asked you along.
I didn't even have a back up plan. Heck, wanna know

Truth is the longer it had me, the more I liked it.
I felt like a child figuring which letters were which,
What added to what made what — it was darn strange.
There were no flashing lights to draw a crowd.
Closest thing I ever saw was a grove of little oranges.

And, after all, it was just me and you. We had listed off
From the group to see if we could get the real nature of it —
The nature of the place where we had no tin shed
To hear the rain ping off of, no yard onions to peel apart,
Nothing but the money talking in our pockets

RIGHT-SIDE OUT

Easy, slow now,
Take what's given from the heart
And the throat of one forgiven
With grace more than precision.
Take care because grudges
Are like canker to the growth
Of you who stand so same-sized
As the tall lines of your adolescence
Marked by the window's darkening
Sash on the jamb of the family door.

Brothers, sisters, cousins, friends —
All gather at the prom that never ebbed,
But grew louder in the shedding
Of tonic chords and parallel fifths,
As measured we all changed partners.
And I heard you hurt a friend, really
Sort of scarred him, by taking
What did not belong to you. But that's
Just a infringement, and one nature
Pinned on you as victim.

It's good to say "I'm sorry"
But only if it's a learning lesson,
And pride will shatter in pieces —
Yours truly, from one who knows.
And yes, love's trinity
May be another glass prism
And in the pure white light that gushes,
You appear all together,
But as we fall off into spaces,
You are left to see the colors

This fist-sized gift
Of rainy day galoshes, and whatever
Else they all left behind.

GREETING OF THE PLAYERS

If we can jolly well hold
Off the crossed staves of the groundlings,
Collect the pieces tossed from the boxes,
And take it all in stride, then the hoax
We live and strive for will soon follow.

Who would think to collect us
In a folio when we're in it just for kicks.
The health of the sick and gouty rich
Is put out for a spell. We assert the noble
Cause of the value in sheer diversion.

And jotting by jot we proof
The text talking to itself again,
Letting loose balloons that rise and float
Into other counties. We tie cards to them
And sometime, postmarked, they return.

JUNE, YOU WERE MY DESIRE

Enough of the peeling and despite the texture —
The inside of the velvet rind our hands lob in the rubbish —
They have restrained us by a piece of blue tape of the floor.

The intern is blonde done in a bun.
She does not wear a scent. She is a professional.
The air she graces becomes its own perfume.

And they are coming soon with the trays.
The others know what time it is and are lining up.
They took away my long hair when I came

Up from the floor where they decided who wasn't right.
But you adapt to the environment: the dark red blood
Drawn by a Japanese nurse.

The tablets drown the drives. Downriver,
Colleagues make love in the margin. You are here
In this pacing place where you talk a little slower, if you talk at all.

MILE OF BAD ROAD

We had been crossed off the list —
Struck from the book of the sandy blue ledger lines
By those who stood in judgment's drawn circle.
At least one of them never thought we would find
Out their names — welders of flaming foils.

But the tree was not in that good a shape, though it might
Regain its foliage before the next episode. The angels were
Too busy raking the fallen leaves
Into yellow piles and hiding in them as if the Word
Was all in fun, small cheer around a scrabble board.

If you follow me, I see no harm in going out
Farther than the good news the manual endorses
And into the field guide topology where
The shining sun is setting. Hold on. I have something stuck
In my throat. Okay. I was talking about us really,
And how to help us get better. I've always been told
You should never tell someone you have a crush on them.

I stopped hanging with their crowd.
They had put an X by your name. I told them
"Well, then count me out too." Violence seethed
Like flames on a grill.
Who ever tried to grow an ungrateful tree
When all these little gray waves keep crashing.

IN THE RISING SUN

Stretching out in the blackberry brakes,
Working elbows and in pairs leaning deep
To gather the bunches so juice full
They look like they might pop and run

In the little scars written deep
In the legacy of our palms and fingers.
No one is brave enough to weave a crown
Out of the thorny twisted legend

And blood legacy. Besides, we've forgotten
Who wore what where with whom in the story.
A day later they would be fetid —
A dizzy mess of flies.

But everything has a schedule.
You and I meet and compare yellow plastic pails.
Yours puts mine to shame,
And as we laugh, our hands touch by accident.

LINES IN BRAILLE

I'd always stayed away
Because of the way you use your silence
Like a grenade tossed in a lobby
Where no one's left to throw themselves
Like a hero in the rushes.
And I knew I would be chosen
For the saving of travelers, wiping
Dry the tears of mothers.
But it was all delusion, a song
Strummed without strings.
Maybe you were a gesture —
Lips mouthing without a voice.
But it's back to the strange
Purpose of your silence even in your rages,
When I walk off the stage adrift
In the echoes of the script —
Mute, yet full of language running
Through my head, our heads.
I'm not sure who is standing behind me
And I'm not sure I want to know.

PETITIONING SPIDERMAN

I asked your mother yesterday
If we could discuss this.
I have not heard back from her.
I would not have you, like me —
A member in the church
In the Congregation of the Nervous.
If you kneel
May you not lose your strength
To anything or anyone outside yourself.
I like the sensitivity you show
When you pat the white cat.
I hope and, yes, pray
No more hardship than you can fend off
Comes your way. This from one
Afraid to sit in the barber's mirror.
I would have you travel
And walk unafraid, though the downpour
May blind, and the conversation
You can't quite make out upstairs,
Turns to abandoned words. So
Follow your heroes.
May they give you the gift
That forgiveness lobs
Like the softball you and I tossed
Last summer
When it was hazy. You caught the ball
And squeezed it for a second
Like it was a prayer
Before you threw it back.

ON THE ADVICE OF A TRUE FRIEND

Postings and cheer
From a basement in Brooklyn USA.
Dressed in black and white, they have their hair.
Next street over color flows past the green signs neatly numbered.

The trees in blossom say
I wear the same shirts too many days in a row. "You don't belong
    here."
The roots conspire. I lose myself in someone I lost — many I lost.
They would reckon I would end up here

Where the upstairs neighbors nettle me bounding on the floor-
    boards,
Tapping in cipher the end of my line.

I am in charge of the furnace. I am the composting champion —
Death seen coming six semis away.

They have me sway towards what can be understood
Without cross or compass. They tug me from the helm.
The floors here are speckled with coins and cigarette burns.
Fruit flies swim around what meaning I reel in from today's vessel.

The maverick, the bounder, the rogue are lodged here.
They would incline to draw me in chalk, stepped on by the children
And washed away at the first spring rain
Without a thought.

SNAGGING A FLY IN THE BLEACHERS

So the kettle has boiled while you were watching it,
Just to test the saying. This does not make you someone other
Than a person who does things to prove people wrong.
Language is lodged in this pocket of the brain, and we can't quite
Launch it off into the puffy clouds like the a toy rocket

You and your father launched behind the bleachers.
You were you a tomboy. It was, and still is, hard to tell
By the way you wear your hair. You like to walk on the beach
Alone in your favorite red sweatshirt.
You are good at getting people hooked on things they'll like.

I spent months in antiquarian bookstores hunting
The exact book on haiku you insisted on in a footnote.
It brought enlightenment just in the turning
Of the fox starred pages   I had satori just mulching the garden.
I gained more tagging all the bases — the water fountains

That kept me alive in Central Park when I was having an episode.
But that was a decade ago. I knew from the "Official Use Only" files
What was a dud and what was actionable. The radio would not
Cease to transmit the frequency you and I had established, nor
Were you an easy lay down by the flowery promenade.

LEMON CHICKEN

The leaves on the sycamore are starting to crinkle again.
I'm on the third floor waiting for you.
If you wake up and knock on my door, I will quit
My showy games and point out where I cut myself shaving.
But you and your troupe are heading back to Europe.
You got the lead role in a play I can't mention, for anonymity's sake.
You disappeared, vanished
Like the woman in a magician's or airliner's black box.
Later you returned to another apartment where I lived
Above you in a fourth-floor walk up. I remember your eyes
like leaden gray veined stained glass of the cathedral —
Pale and with that funny tooth.   I was a fool not to run
My fingers through your hair.   But I was enamored
By your neighbor who was hot on your roommate in love's raffle.
You didn't quite invite my touch when we climbed
The wooden ladder up to the tar and tin roof. I would give up blue
    skies
To have a second chance in the night's drizzle.
I can't tell who is dropping whom
And who keeps whom beside them in the red, lambent glitter.
It came after you left — like a note echoing on a seven second
Delay mechanism. I put flowers on the mantel.
The room was strung out with thin gauge magic wires
Designed to ward off omens and keep the yellow petals
From falling farther down into eternity.

FRENCH AND ENGLISH SUITES

What is there in me that wishes I would crash —
That this episode would make last time look like amateur work.
But no, I stay in control on autopilot in the sunbeams.
Tomorrow's headlines will be the same as today's.
The woman will give birth to another skunk —

As if it isn't enough to get confused listening to the BBC
Though headphones, to conflict and clerics I don't recognize.
This textual entity is me taken to a taxidermist and stuffed,

Set in a corner of the room so my friends can be frightfully
Panicked to see it was true. I did come back.
Children dressed in back and white are playing hopscotch
Under the eye of the Master of the Universe.

When I walk by on the sidewalk
Their mothers call them in behind the chain link fence.
There are voices in the house I can't make out.
And I wonder if it's Russian — the laughter of the mother
Footnotes my basement apartment around supper.

I wonder what it's like to land in a plane and know
You have left everything and everyone behind.

My back is bad. I will have to take a pill.
I press hard into the chair, which helps the pain.
And I'm sorry to say I must be going.
The cell is buzzing and my copilot's voice
Will bring me down on Cortelyou Street. Now and here,
When I don't understand what is happening to me
And hope she is drinking coffee in her usual haunts.

YOU WHO NEVER WERE

Back, way back when,
I wanted to visit you at dusk
When the rain was talking softly,
And your wicker basket
Overflowed with apples.

Then we "Wished each other well"
And fell into the loops —
The lemon gin of pick-up joints
And no talking to strangers on the F trains.
Society bars random connections.

Outside, at least, the fall
Was dropping its petals, blossoms,
And sycamore leaves. Small dogs
Cruised through the wet streets.
My shoes went squish squish squish.

I saw you in the dead
Mannequins in Midtown, dressed
In the sheer colors the way you liked
When summer had come and gone
Like a stranger, handing you a gun.

A RUINED HOUSE

I can still hear his voice
From the house beneath honeysuckle
Blanketed by the light of the sickle moon.
I was pledged to always watch over him
In the prayers he was starting to pray.
On Cortelyou Road where we had been shopping, he held
My hand as we came to a sidewalk stoplight.

He cried out when the soap got in his eyes,
But what could I do: the kid's gotta get a bath.
Toys scattered everywhere in my ex's apartment,
Dishes filling the sink left for me to wash
On my evenings when I picked him up from nursery school.
He drew his monsters
With a crow black magic marker he had lost the top for.
He had to draw quickly before the marker
Dried up like childhood.

Because he asked nicely from under the vines,
I gave him twenty minutes of TV. Then I vanished.
The creed was kept   He was no longer scared of the monsters
Roving. They couldn't romp through the raspberry prickles.
I planted the bushes when he was born, thinking it would
Be an activity. But the ruins of the old basement
Were taken by the kudzu like happens in the South
Where my family comes from.
And I couldn't say a word to stop it.
It was, as lawyers say, an act of god.

A FIG TREE GROWING WILD

The twist is beginning —
The neighbors' hello each other between houses
Where the lawns compete, and magical flowers
Hide the mushrooms the college kids hunt out.

Once you dilate, you are committed
To giving life to the growing light.
Saints are in agreement,
As is the doctor in a three floor Tudor house.

His boys hide coolers on the paths
On paths in the boxwoods.
There's a fox makes home there —
A creek where when you turn stones,

Crayfish scoot out.
The new father is listing to the Unfinished Symphony.
Never mind the bollocks that suck suburbia dry
As a velvet vest.

A WORD FROM OUR SPONSORS

The program won't open in this font.
You can understand. You made it with chicken wire.
That's not a common use.
You get me, Private?
It was just sitting there rusting after the war
Forced us to go normal.

What the hot thing is now is cassette players.
We must have our music and since the net
Is now down. We have batteries and tapes
We hunt out in the shells of secondhand stores
Like madmen searching for Easter eggs.

Did I say that? Or did you think it back to me
From an unknown point in the future.
Are you alive? Do you need to use the restroom?
You lean differently depending on what's at stake.

But your rank does not allow you leeway
To go off base and use your sticky fingers
To get D-cell batteries at the 99 cent store
So you can make your companion's toy run.

Besides, I was trying to duck and hide not far away.
We're not at work in the same time synch —
Central saw that coming and restricted me to nonsense.
And so it goes. And so it will go.
And the past is always hungry to gobble up the now.

THE STEAKHOUSE

How could I know you were on the other side —
That you were not an enemy and not a friend, but a warm body
That caved in when the guests spoke of higher culture.

You carried your lump of bills taped behind your knee,
And all my uncouth friends kept asking me if I'd tapped you yet.
Yeah. Yeah. Yeah. It's not like I wouldn't like to.

There's not a heaven singing over the pricks of the hedges
Of the slovenly basement apartment where I sleep in the daytime.

When someone rings me up or texts me, I am given to dreams
Of being in a sandbox — no, I mean a sandbox for grown ups
And your hosing down my feet to get rid of all the grit.

We can't have sand getting on Ma Ma's Turkish rugs.
And I would wear my shoes inside her trappings, but I
Lost them somewhere in the dream of the open road.
Here the road is closed. You have to tip everyone.
Mavericks live alone and polish their Harley sleds.

They say they've never had a wreck. Never lost a fight.
And the tattoos on their arms cost them the country club.

RAT'S NEST

They did it in 8mm
For sickos on the way
To the precinct.
In Mexico, where life
We think is cheap.
But that was what '69,
'70 and showed
In musty makeshift theaters
'Cause that was the law
Talking. My 8th grade
History teacher glossed
It and wiped his glass.
He said they'd get a drunk
And roll him out where
No one would miss him.
Must have been some money
In it — or something else:
The need to stripe evil
On someone else.
In London during
Charles and Diana's wedding,
I stayed soused on Strongbow cider
And made a German woman.
That's about it. If you are into
True Crime or methods
Of interrogation and torture,
Look away.
You might look like anyone else.
But my friend is busy
Stringing surveillance
Cameras round the city.
I asked him if he was

Investigating me.
Naw, he said, popped
The cherry on the dashboard,
And laughed.

RAIN IN APRIL

What we lose in fluidity we gain in subject matter —
Unless we truly lose like the girl spinning a bucket of water
Who stops and gets drenched. This is a progress that
We must always going at full tilt. If we stop a day
The parts rust over. If only it were just plain talking,
The guide might not make us paint our faces and stop catching
Lightening bugs in a mayonnaise jar. This is a nurse shark:
It must keep moving or it will die. It is a marathon
Made of many sprints all strung along.

So it's death do us part. We've tried to keep vows,
But the situation caved in. Only memory of the ritual,
The words, and the signatures linger. We misplaced
The playbill that told us what roles we were playing.
And it's daily news that the show does not always go on.

Somewhere along the line the "we" split. There was
A "you" and "I." That was the saddest day in life.
This now is a dig — an excavation — of remembered times together,
Both the good and the bad, the spring rain and the winter slush.
What was once pure, white snow went from gray to black
Like the simple way we treated each other.
I saw you slipping on the sidewalk covered with ice.
I tried to grab you before you fell and fell myself.
Now we keep separate residences, although I still tune in
To the radio talk shows you got me hooked onto.
Somewhere along the line, the bucket stopped spinning.

MORBID DREAD

Does anyone else feel a draft in here —
Or is it just me? The clients judge by the silliest thing.
They'll be perfectly nice to your face is the thing.
Ok. Are the sculptors here with the ice swan? Good.
That's what I want here, but I'm still not sure
About the mistletoe. Is there some religious thing
Attached to mistletoe? No? It's a seasonal,
Secular emblem?   I dittoed the opening speech
They used last year … On second thought, no mistletoe.
I don't want to give off the wrong idea. This is not
A romance; it's a symposium. Anything else going on,
Keep it in your hotel room. The blue streamers are good.
Who came up with the blue streamers? Whoever is was,
Nice touch. And who's the captain of the catering
Team? Jason? Well, ok. Just watch the white wine.
He's a lush, and this German stuff the sommelier picked
Ain't cheap. Lemme tell you.   See to it Jason doesn't stash away
A bottle. Is the CEO coming? Or was that rumor?
Ok. Ok. Folks. The cars are pulling up. Show time.

A MAGICAL DREAM

I guess I've always had feelings and emotions —
That metal glint you can see in the eyes.
Mostly, I have downplayed them or been less than honest
In what I do to keep from killing someone or

Burying my head in the sand.
Bad stuff happens, and I try to brush it off.
Other times, something good comes my way.
I take this as a flashing yellow

That I'm about to be in collision. I'm never prepared
For the next move. But I have learned my friends
And my enemies are touchstones by which I test my metals.
Sometimes a friend flashes as an enemy and vice versa.

Stunning me with unasked for insight, I recognize the truth.
I'm not big on self-discovery. As a rule,
It hurts. But I learn to awaken my own self-approval
In obeying the lessons the wise demonstrate.

A PLACE TO BE

Those were places to visit — open vistas and sunken gardens.
I made them because I needed to feel good about myself.
They were meant as gifts wrapped in red paper and tied off
With a ribbon. What more can they do than offer distraction?

I look at life, but I can't offer any moral guidance. Chew before
You swallow is about the best I can do. This one is up front.
Just to see the banner of what you really think is truth following
Me past the rusty track to the pond where we look at the ducks.

Nature has its own way, even if it's not a method. Things just go.
Watch the ducklings trailing behind the mother. And what chaos
Speaks of its design signs off on this thesis before its defense.
I can only speak of experience — this fugitive of the fishes.

A diving bell is fun, but it's scary. I think of my own life as one
Long spell underwater. It's not my element.
And when those in the boat above decide it's time for me to come up,
I know when I reach the surface my lungs will burst.

AN OCCASIONAL POEM

Talk to me. I'm all ears. Now that we have some time alone.
I thought the meeting was going to go on forever. And she had the
     nerve
To say that she thought there was going to be wine. Lately,
It's been all voices. The image of my ex blots out the windows
Where I used to see the whitetail deer feeding then looking up.

Like I was saying, this "medium" is from Romania. She's pale
With very white skin and dark hair. Now let me tell you something.
I think he was seeing her before we split. He had the nerve
To call it therapy. I found a bag he'd hidden away in the closet.
It was full of candles and little bottles of red and purple liquid.

When I confronted him, he said it was part of the therapy.
"You're the one who said I needed to see someone."
At first I was angry. Then I was hurt. I felt like a doll
He had dropped on the slate path and had broken off an arm.
He wiped away my tears reeking from her cheap perfume.

LONG LOOK INTO NIGHT

This is the night of the forty-watt bulb,
When the heart can't tell itself how it should feel.
The light is still too bright for what the heart holds.
I am showing myself what hurts. People hurt,
People and places and things hurt.
They carry the still abiding past. Take a sled —
One you used as a child. Rust has grown over
The runners you used to wax. And the hill
You sled down seems part of a conspiracy.
It is part of a whole and one of many more.
The lesser angels with wings of gauze
Have given up on hoisting the pulley
That lifts god's lost into a darkening heaven.
You came here without a reason to come.
You stayed here without a reason to stay.
You will leave here without a reason to leave.
You stare at the forty-watt bulb
Until it, like your wakefulness, seems to fade
Into the early hours of the morning
When you lose what you were looking for
And find what you never meant to find.

THE FRONDS

In the cattails
They walked with their flashlights.
One shined his beam
In a place neither
Land nor water.
He pointed his light
To show the other the clear jelly
Asleep with a thousand eyes.
From these
Will come a thousand frogs.
Give or take a few.
The pair left
Their wives and families,
To go gigging in the dark. One left
His gig on the moss bank
To stare through the rushes.
The smaller man cradled
A thin spear with three barbed points.
All at once, the glare
Of the flashlight fell on a frog
And nudged it off its lily pad.
"Too far anyways," the larger man said.
"Too early in the season."
As if it wasn't right with God,
Lightning struck over the tree line.
"Damn," the smaller one said,
Admiring the power
Of nature's arsenal.
Then the rain picked up quickly.
"Come on," the larger one said.
"I left the window
On the truck down."
But before he finished speaking

A bolt of lightning struck
Halfway down the length of a pine tree.
The rest was tumult —
A curdling scream that lasted
But a breath.
It broke the man's back
A few notches from the nape.
It was the larger man who told
His friend's wife.
She pummeled his chest and cried in the glare
Of the flashing ambulance lights.
OK, It's Later

As I read through her pages,
They take on many meanings and none at all.
As for her art, I love it for its imperfections.
If it were perfect,
I would feel like I was in a cage.

I sense her influences.
She writes as if captive in a sunny breeze.
Many moments make me pause.
But that's the game,
And whatever they say, it's no small thing.

I don't want this house to eat its young,
But once you hop down from the tree
It's hard to get the bird off your shoulder.
You must resort to these tricks
To keep the bird from seeing its shadow.

DRIVING THROUGH THE GROVE

Let me give you an example: my reputation
Was as a van — almost new, low mileage. And I woke up
One afternoon to find some nice people spray-painted
Tags all over it, keyed the sliding door, and drove a nail
Through a rear tire. Now I am considering getting out
Of this state of mind in which I find myself.

I don't mean I want to buy some well-to-do place,
And I don't want to bad mouth anyone —
Not even the nice people who made caca of my good name.
I'm talking assisted living. Ever since the separation,
I've secretly wanted someone to help —
Someone to help make things easier on me.

It's hard enough living without a drink.
Harder still to see my son only twice a week.
I want to return to the part of the museum that had
Soutine's swaying streets and Picasso's cubist femmes.
I walk through the rooms in my basement apartment
And think in all the mess, there must be a floor here somewhere.

Nick and I had a good night,
But I felt sick from nerves and drinking
A twenty-ounce energy drink
On top of my usual Klonopin.

I couldn't get on the subway to his school.
I shelled out a twenty to go there and back.
Once I was with my son, the nerves
Eased and I felt more myself.

We went to the usual spot
And had iced pink herb tea
And two bowls of macaroni and cheese.
He was on good behavior, and I texted

His mother that he was back to his self.
I suspect he badtalks me to his playmates,
But it's been tough, tough on him especially.
I'm scared if I shook him, a piece would rattle.

PARASITE

You feel
You're about
To cough
April's chill
Again back
In bed at noon.
No lover,
No other
To get medicine.
This is what
You get
For loving
Poorly, for
Living poorly.
This is a spine,
And this disc
Has slipped
Out of place
Forever.
You start
To pray
Mouthing,
Trembling
Under the sheet
Wound around you,
As though
You were a worm
Invading a host.

NECESSARY CONDITIONS

The jitters are timeless.
Walking by the hill, you see her shut her door,
And you don't know if she saw you,
And was trying to tell you to keep walking.
The lows come and go.
They live in eternity, reaching out
Of time. They have no friend.
They are as a white sail taut in the wind —
Full as the belly of a drunkard.
Their edge can cut like an ice skate
The lazy 8 of infinity when she chooses
To lie down of the icy plank
Sideways. The captain is lost in star-charts.
The compass spins, but spins
Slowly as a man's hand reaching
For coins in a dream.
They move farther out
Of reach. The grasp of his winks
Are crabs on the beach. The shore itself
Is a dream where dark figures
Are in every window —
Mannequins who cannot dream,
The purple and yellows of their dressings —
And things that conspire, and that's all.

AFTER THE WAR

All the raindrops fall like words.
They don't mean you any harm.
But I see you looking out your window,
And woman you don't look happy.

Is the crucifix you hold out
Meant to drive me off?
Or does it signify something you hold deep
And a totem I must share

If I would talk to you
In the room you rent and sweep
The dust that falls through the night.
You wash your feet in a basin

And look in your small, wood-framed mirror.
In a lassitude, you go to the window
Where, pausing, I glimpse your face
Through a window box of crimson flowers.

THE ST. CROIX MIX

You entered by the way most people don't use
Not only because of fear, but also because they don't see any point.
The people you met by the pool were friends.
You trusted them to have a grudge against Columbus and his painted
    vessels.
The place we honeymooned had a brass plaque saying
In this very spot he touched down and harbored.

We were in love. I watched you draw in pastels on the sunny deck.
We ate at all the recommended restaurants the island had to offer.
The acrimony was nascent and in a natal stage. It was all sand I
    forgot
To wash off my feet in the syndrome and disorder you triggered.
    Later, you
Used everything against me in a lawyer's office for a cool glass of
    water and
Signatures in triplicate.

I hide them, but I have feelings. I am always looking back.
The snares of the past are both a trap and an announcement by drum
    roll.
Some canceled episodes are going to run at midnight.
This is the stinging nettle as well as the honeysuckle and mint
I came to know in your garden. I came to know some plants you
    called
Weeds because your friends decided they were weeds.

LAKE BY ST. CHARLES

So you just switched it on autopilot while you watched the ducks.
You laughed at the drake mallard busy putting on a show on the lake.
I know. I was playing my part too, walking with my girlfriend
Who wanted to go back to the car for some bread to feed the
    waterfowl.
I thought you were going to break up with me beside that lake.
A friend of yours I'm partial to let it slip this morning.

I should have been a stuntman. But not one in the real world.
I would be a mental stuntman thinking the unthinkable, imagining
    what
No one dared imagine. You always said I was deranged, but in a
    funny,
Giggles way. You said I placed too much weight on coincidence
That morning after waffles and syrup in the diner in the Quarter.
I can't figure how a hot number even ended up with a dunce.

I guess that duck was pretty happy with you feeding him slices of
    bread.
You had a regular congregation gathering and quacking as you dished
    out
Out the entire loaf, piece by piece. We were having fun again, and
    you took
My hand in yours. And the hen favored the drake and all was well.
Walking back to your dorm, you confessed you had thought of break-
    ing up,
But the light in the live oaks made things good and sane in its
    falling.

WILLIAMSBURG

It's true I was drowsy
Behind the wheel, the signs
Said I was getting
Closer to your sprawling
College town. I was there
And then, nowhere
In the headlights speeding
Toward someone I had
Never forgotten. People
Drop out of your life, like
Pills spilled on linoleum.
When you're on your knees
Praying to the god
Of tranquilizers to gather
Each and every one.
And it seems I'm going
Nowhere. It is my age.
The miles on the signs
Are growing higher.
I am dreaming. I am dancing
With you in my arms.
I am free to drop
Coins when putting on my pants.
I am free, you say, to go ahead
And shower. The sky has been
Over me in its summer heat,
And I have a funk on me.
But you will still say no.
You will water the plants
And ignore I am running
My fingers through your hair.
I knew the rules
As soon as you let me in.

And God is deaf and dumb
In this dream on I-64
When I fail to wake
From my dream,
Nodding as if to say "Thank you."

A TREE IN THE BREEZE

Anything could pull me closer
To you now — the scythe of a capital "C" —
An owl over a field of winter wheat.

You are the farthest east that east can go —
Your ethics overcome our plentiful morality.
We fear the folded flag may never be whisked up.

You are bountiful in the sway of your handbag.
You promises are as the setting sun. Your old books
Are full on the ancient emperors' likenesses.

This is abstract, but not an abstraction.
There is no black like the black of your hair.
Love, beware. They'll crash through these paper screens.

TENURE

Poison runs down your back the way it was in the desks.
You passed notes — oh, such nasty, curt seepages encircling
The unpopular girl who had yet to grow taller.
Grubs in the lot disgusted you, hundreds of white grubs.

You say I'll meet you behind the bleachers after demerits.
You turn on the rest of your skunk reeking crew
And the boys bonding with a chew of tobacco at the bench.
How juvenile they were: pickers of noses — spitting brown.

Sitting in a brick cove you blew gray smoke in "O"s —
One ring through another, like the rings of your mother
Working on her third marriage, which has set up camp
In the quiet disorder of the boys rounding the corner.

You have urges, and you give in. You purge to keep thin.
You cut up once, but that was a fad of cells beckoning.
And now you instill fear. Now you make marks of correction
Blinking at all the innocent faces seated neatly in rows.

20.5 POEMS

1.

The zones of your smile lose me —
The way you wring your hands
During this sad first episode,
Which nobody, save me, can follow.

But let's not get into all that.
Your chestnut mare has been stabilized.
People have forgotten, kind of.
You're still the champ of darts in the village.

Baby's breath bed all thirteen roses,
Which are the secret marks of the day.
They open the door to the wild outside,
And your father goes with us to your apt.

Even the cache of dusty vinyl records
You left scattered is neatly in a row.
You want to make love,
But realize the white cat is missing.

2.

And you were the only one
Left sultry, sulking in the stands —
Bits thrown and spilled by the departed
Surround you like a handful of stray stars.

Once the astral camera zoomed in
To catch the moony crescent of your cheekbone,
And dwelling on the screen I remembered
You showing me your fillings back to the molars.

I came down with something — ached all over.
Even the corner boys couldn't help me,
And you called me a faker
Before you kissed my lips and was out the door.

How could I know I would never see you
Come home after you were God knows where,
With God knows whom doing God knows what?
Your glistening belly spoke louder than lies.

3.

The Department of Transport ripped off
The dolphin tweaking in the tank —
You say they follow you unmasked
Deeper into this poem using sonar on cars.

The bleeping, my love, I can hear as well,
But what is signified I can't tell.
Subcompacts trailing you, tailing you
Force my hand to bear down on this page.

I still pray to sleep with your back
Against me, curved like the f-holes
Of the guitars they play down in Smalls —
The club where you went tonight in the rain.

You say they used sonar to follow you home —
Second-guessing survey of your surveillance:
Swelling sine waves, love, all over the West Village
And you shook your blind umbrella like an asp.

4.

The song kept popping up
Like kids from leaf piles.
And this opacity is nylon
Like the tents where we were laughing.

So we rollicked under a shattered moon.
Amidst the field of green tassels,
The melody that became "Our Song"
Some strummer was picking.

"God, can you imagine," you said
In the morning. "What it would
Have been like if we had actually met —
Caught up in hours, boxcars, and cake."

A mosquito whined in my ear.
The sun was rising over the crop.
I could not tell
Whether it was dew or frost.

5.

Blonde with an easy manner, you lean
Deep into the films of a romance,
Making textual notes not to share with me and her.
We have no common ground to stand upon.

Ribbons before you fall off into the bells —
You sink a low ball in a corner pocket.
Love, you are a pinball machine stuck on tilt.
You are something on the side, but you don't mind.

Dean of strawberries, my ultra pale —
Petals, silver peelings, number of secret love,
Mysterious gainsayer, Asst. Chair of the everything,
Whom I glimpse in an act hard to follow.

Never know — life throws a mean curve
That seems to float just over the bleachers
Of clouds and clichés. I tease myself
Imagining the rolls of dream would click on us.

6.

And here I am in love with your book.
You laugh. I don't let my birth name out to anyone.
But the house for unwed mothers
Had covered her name and so here I am

Carrying some wine and thirteen roses
To your doorstep where I buzz and hear you screaming.
The kitchen was full of smoke. There was
A grease fire on the burner we put out.

"My hair is greasy," you said. "And dinner's all burnt."
Their cats ate it from a china dish. But we still had green beans.
"Fire's out —— Thank God." Why didn't you
Tell me you were adopted?"

Was it David or Dah-Veed? Guess it doesn't make much difference.
But I'm more of a David now. Of course your David.
I talk in my sleep and wait patiently for the Lord
To raise me from this mire and establish my goings.

7.

All I can do is say sorry. A synthesis
Of cloud cover and a checkered shepherd's check jacket
Lured the moon's penumbra of a bitter taste.
Scared, I felt shame, then took it back.

My vow I would never veer — all my spelling words
Were two years from last Tuesday a year back.
Cutting it on the mirror, I caught my reflection
See the jawing of how I lost you.

Taking showers together never really works,
But the beads of water on your back
Streamed down, over your nape.
A lost tossed dossier and pearls and you were gone.

You took a year in the shower and then dressing
With the tiger-year pendant listing as you bent over.
I tried to kiss you. How could I know
I would forever see you again.

8.

Shards of slate I swerved around
As you popped your gum in 8mm film —.
"BEWARE OF FALLING ROCKS" and "DEER CROSSING."
I like your grainy projection on my screen.

I hadn't taken it out in year, but it worked
And caught the honey dripping from the spoon —
The spoon you bent out of habit.
The mountain road glittered diamond

Like the ring I gave you, you wore on your thumb.
From the overlook, I could see the river run,
The missile silo, and a red tailed hawk.
You stayed down reading over and over:

"DO NOT ENTER." Your drawn blood
Made you unafraid. You fingered the orbits
Of a deer's skull, and nodded in a nosebleed.
Bootless you slipped off Hell's red pony.

9.

What are you blind to do? They prize the pelts
Of burning tigers sinning 'round the West Village.
Our friends have dressed us in camouflage and gas masks —
Rogues in a red silk room, windows of the night.

The mannequins are sultry falsetto in Cowgirls Hall of Fame.
The cop is trying not to perjure a nasty little incident,
You lounge by the bookstall and remember the feel of books.
You could read letters in red that was the blood.

You say it looks like I'm riding an ass. You
Tap your white cane. People differ only by proximity.
You see a elder couple crossing Hudson,
"If only I could see the suffering people live with."

O this thin context doesn't end and leaves us lost.
But come spring we can go punting together anon.
They think we work for the government,
And who is to say? You brush out your long, blown hair.

10.

I spent an hour shouting at your car.
It budge it did not budge.
Finally, you rapped on my window.
I yelled. "Hey, Buddy, can't you see I'm stuck!"

They had only called for flakes and sprinkles.
My hands were numb & I was late to pick her up.
I can see she her tizzy now, telling me
There was no way we would make it to the show.

But I got by the truck
When I buzzed your door you were humming.
I have a surprise:
I'm pregnant.

One phrase could undo my life like a ball on twine.
"Have you told anyone?" I asked.
This is the most wonderful day of my life.
"You are certain you have not told anyone?"

10.5.

I spent a hour shoveling out your car,
Throwing down salt to be good to the neighbors.
My shovel broke just when you called me in.
Halleluiah to busted shovels.

You had only called me to roll up a rug —
And my fingers were numb, and something in my back
Said "You need a couple shots of single malt."
But you bodily stopped me as I opened the cabinet.

"You said the shoveling was the last thing I had to do."
"So I have to hold true to my word and you don't."
What? "I know about the babysitter. She told me."
"I haven't the faintest what you're talking about."

"Go. Get back to it. Shovel the neighbors, Shovel the
Whole damn block. You won't be living here long."
"The babysitter lied. "And the last one, and the one
Before her?" "I'm filing the papers tomorrow, Bub."

11.

The remains of the sun are scattered in Alphabet City:
The vintage jeans, the junky jungle shirt from the 60s.
And the white silk gloves up to your elbow you and
Your sticky fingers walked past the cashier wearing.

I had to swipe you with my card to get us home.
Delancey had a new mosaic that looked like an aquarium,
And we, my impossible goldfish, passed where I used to record.
The songs are not the in scene, but I'd give them time.

Do you remember the oranges talking to the wind?
Me neither. You had your boyfriend then,
But the bond was breaking — over.
I touched your long, slurry curls. "No," you said.

You were not mine yet. You slid on your new gloves
From the pocketbook you had lifted from a street vender.
"I'm sorry," you said. "I don't know where my head is at."
And I knew that moment you forever would be mine.

12.

I was born a camera. You were watercolor.
You painted our wall with sticks and stones.
I threw pillows all over the place.
Our venue went out and had an episode.

I became obsessed after you left me.
All I would eat for a month was meat.
I saw flyers of you heading events in Manhattan.
I was not jealous, jealous, or even jealous.

So I went. You sidled up and in my ear
Said "You really need to work on your game."
I replied "Someone's out to make a vaccine
Against you." You smiled and blinked

And smiled and blinked some more.
Wasted, Lord, on a stunning young woman.
It was all wasted on the both of us —
Me, the zero card you spread on the table.

13.

Time to huck a rock into time's garden.
And as the gray, angelic rain starts to fall,
In my steel boots, my lucky chamois shirt, we
Encounter this: an instance of the symboliste.

It is not popular, but may win out.
Not quite opaque, not transparent — let us call
This the aesthetic of the translucent. It opens
Into the ontological, sometime sideway into the barn.

That place, the farm, was the last place I saw Nancy,
Floating in an inner tube out by the float
Where thieves kept bolt-cutting the chain
That kept the rowboat that was our joy.

See these can be real, too. I won't forget Nancy,
How her legs were slathered with sunscreen.
How everything about this revision
Is a signature written in wine.

14.

I have written you down two times.
Both times the save function failed and you
Will never be who you were
In the sparkling nails of your first incarnation.

All I have are the marks in the grass
Where your bare feet swift-footed ran
While your mother tried to call you into the cage
As if you were a songbird.

I feel much better now. The document has saved
Three times in a row. You are no longer
The young woman I knew in the first draft.
This is you, but you with body paint —

A textual entity whose hand once I held,
Part of the triangle whose bright ting sharpens
The evening, stills evening air. You are smart.
I fear the games with surgery will awaken your heart.

15.

Since the accident I sleep to wake —
Lo! In delirium. You guidest me back
Away from the fireplace, away from
The pair of dueling pistols in Act II.

Who are you? You have my wedding ring.
Am I your ——? Husband?
You hang another IV bag.
I push the button for the pain.

All of your hands are blurred.
It is as if there were two of you.
No! There are two.
I am forever to be tended to by a lovely pair.

So be it, as it was, selah!
Forever involved with a pair in my pain.
Who am I today? I must be someone.
You...excuse me, pardon me, but...

16.

In the box you fill in your name, age, and other information —
Like Lord Jim you feel your past zero.
They can't catch how the manner of your dance is changing.
All they want to know is where you were when and with whom.

True, true. I would add your voice is growing quieter
Ever since the riot of your age wrecked itself out of sorts.
Agreed: it's hard to know which button to push nowadays.
But you are lucky: God graced you with common sense.

"It's just me: the same girl you remember floating
Out too far at the beach." I remember you getting the sand
Off your feet in the cottage shower, trying to catch
The lizard in Captiva, constantly on the lookout where we

Spanned the bridge for dolphins. But now you've grown
Silent, like the woman you are in explicit solitude.
You said, "No. I'm never lonely when they, even you,
With your brown books and scuba gear, disappear."

17.

Now stretching full height, you want to accessorize.
Behind your back they mock you —
It may be a cultural thing as the officer on duty
Tries to trip you into incriminating yourself.

Dalliances and daytrips out to the country house:
Freshened us.   Now you make a face working out a kink
In your shoelace. In some other sphere or precinct,
You sit down and order you wardrobe online.

Finally, the guests arrive! O the sight of you
In a crimson sweater, their very eyes dilate.
Tripping: someone points at a pastel cat,
Which turns to be a crumpled frock as we regain our senses.

And I don't think your secret is so safe.
Crossing the border, the officers are asking questions.
About you, our friends, the Swiss tree house
We had commissioned back when, in another life.

18.

Listen. Can't you see she's in pain?
She wasn't wanted by her own mother —
Either of them. The one who raised her
Stayed locked in her room ignoring the voices,

Or the one who gave her up —
A legal name, a birthmark, and zilch else.
The society paper was printed in red that day,
And all the rectors developed a hunchback and limp.

Grown, she licked the habits her doctor blew
Like a bassoon, and awoke to find herself a flute.
This is why the knot was tied in the first play —
The Original Know of her conception,

Although some people gainsay her origins —
It was all like arguing about a summer storm.
Now grown into a curve
We lean and laugh at the hats in all the boxes.

19.

Two gazelle go wild, each with its own game, or orbit —
Opening wrappers unto the wind.
And pure, they turn to deciding which niche on restraint row.
They mock each other about their raspy tongues.

Pets of a menagerie, imported from everywhere:
They stare like blood stars as they are ushered into nowhere.
Small brown bats flutter in the evening heavens,
Malingering like a rumor over Manhattan.

Chewing on taffy from the shore, I have lost my friends.
I lost them when I went to get my dry cleaning done —
Trusting my camelhair, camouflaged long coat to strangers.
It's a game. The algorithms inspire, call the role of the dice,

Determine the tiny black eyes of my mice, the outcome of games
In the garden, the topiary giraffe, the run of ivy on a brick wall, and
Keeping all this out of the reality games the gazelle is stuck on.
Even as a kid, I could never keep my laces tied.

20.

Goat, gray, cold, forever stag — drab days they feed me
Rusty cans, rotten cabbage, other peelings of the night.
They need me — half pet, half a laugh of utility, the rubbish
Of a wing-ding clam bake where everyone sneaks off.

That way the drowsy cuckold basks in gauzy firelight.
Before I was changed, she took a brute who hoisted boxes.
Goat is a laugh: a charcoal scribble of a child.
For fun they never call me the same name twice.

Thus, identity is obscured. I am Goat.
I chew dry ice in the ring of daffodils.
I am beyond all hope of the flask of easy conversation.
Many years back, I was a white lamb, nice lamb.

Now I watch the two that once were mine dancing.
They are as darkly fetching as words can render them.
At least my non-words, the bleatings of Goat,
Will call higher law to sort things out. Thinkest Goat.

CAREFREE AND
COMELY

RULES OF TEMPTATION

It's when this Sunday evening light
Starts to get to you. Nowhere
And no time, between yesterday and today,
Night and day, this week and next
And neither of us is with the one we love
Fit close to one in a mountain retreat.

Still, life goes on behind and between the lines.
They are on my mind again, Dear Diary,
And the high voltage lines run over the pond.
Where once your chosen played in the open.
Now the war is in full swing.
The little red bats are a source for organizations,

And the new design the team contrived
Leaves no signature. We rely on the Constitution
Wherever the powers station us.
We get off singing to the trails of stars.
You are always in the adjacent room — that we know —
Reading a magazine, wringing your hands in the dark.

AIRPORT MAN

That's what you call tight security —
And all the broaches beneath your leather vest:
The no question medals of the organization.

Even the footsteps you left were hot.
At 20,000 feet you experienced enlightenment, satori.
Staring at the tip of your nose.

The topmost yoga of Krsna —
The all attractive one. You wanted to chant,
But the organization would frown.

You've gone polytheistic, mad, and order a drink.
You consume eight little bottles of vodka.
The clouds were woven white and puffy.

LOTTERY DUNCE

New loves and boxcar machinery
Can carry heavy cargo.
Let's hope for rain this week
The corn is calling for it.
The yellow stalks begin to bend.

And the one you are thinking of
Has an agenda where you play a random role
Together under the water tower,
You lay together in the dry grass
The moon strange and radish red.

That morning the rain begins,
But someone's gone missing
Someone's nowhere to be found.
"Thank you for listening" murmurs the ground
And in silence returns to sleep.

VALENCES

Darkness in these worlds.
Light to write by.
Forty-watt.

Not the darkness of lizards,
But that of a clean room.
Mockingbird at night.

The darkness the child knows.
Cards splayed in a flush
Under the casino table.

And the greenbacks beg
To be pressed in a gold clip
By a map of eviscerated promises

To drive by at night
In the black rain
Only the blind can see.

AT FORTY

She is all smiles in the box of your mind —
Legs crossed and laughing at your dry sense,
And like your last love her favorite fruit is lemon.
You imagine the night she will first dress in red.

You excuse yourself to the latrine
And when you come back she is gone.
On the table there's an open book of matches
On which is written the words "GO HOME."

CIRCLE OF CATS

Black leopard, patchy, hungry.
The younger edge the better of the kill.

She draws a colorful card for me
Of a wildcat's torn identity.

She is pale. She's rules me out.
She shakes my tree for cash.

Flirting with the prayers,
Meddling with her astral patterns.

They tell me just when I give out
Someone will join me at the table.

Beckon me to return their serve
And pick at their sweet spot with my nails.

I see she's got game. That she's lonely
And turns the tarot's zero Fool's Card.

She taught me to take her slowly —
If only I could remember who I am.

INVITE

Yes, I retreat — say and gainsay —
Tie and untie the pawn's shoelace.

Purpose? What Purpose? Hide, I say.
Hide one and go on to the next.

If I am to die, let me die like snow
In a gang of yellow flowers

Or the gradually loudening voice
Or a lady drinking a dirty martini —

Softening and hardening
With crimson toenails just done

Let me die with memory and with glitter —
This tickertape of God, my life.

SOME LINES CROSSED OUT

Let's step inside because of the weather.
This downpour is out of season. The drops
Sting your face in a sympathetic fallacy.
Your double is in a constant pose
Behind the shop plate glass. We go bar
To the bar getting hammered at brunch.

To be frank, if we weren't such good friends
I'd turn you into a play where I was the villain.
If you were deployed, I'd be your comfort
And move in and out of a shared nostalgia:
"The Man Whose Woman lived in the display window."
"Amnesia on 5th Ave."

Sometimes I go to see you move like an automaton.
I let my mind play tricks. Hell. What's the difference?
It takes a peel and eat unsound mind to pull off
These provocative arrangements
On the F train, dripping wet, out of sorts,
Standing, holding the pole when no one's in sight.

UNCONTROLLABLE LAUGHTER

I'm sorry that I called you a mannequin.
You've been nothing but kind to me.
But let's drop it — let bygones be bygones.

This is a job for imagery: you in your sequins
Scrubbing the grease out of the pot
Left from the Coney Island Mermaid Parade.

There's a catch of mussels that fell behind the stove
That we can't get out. Even the divine son's
Velvet portrait does not empower us so.

We know couples in confusion and confrontation —
Couples who argue about who will scrub the pot.
I'm sorry — I'm laughing. This is too funny.

THE PUPPY'S TAIL

They cut the lock to free this love.
Someone's riding it around or else
Someone's ravaged it for parts.

What's next? My shoes?
My significant other's prosthetic limb?
Is nothing sacred?

All the lessons I took at an early age
Amount to beans. All my medical charts
Spread across the parking lot

Of the Code Blue world,
And a hole just wore through
My jeans back pocket.

And my time to brave the wind is pouring
Out into the small pile of time
I have left to find a patch.

WORRIES

How am I to OM?
With this head full of fretfulness?

Thoughts enter and exit, mix and move
All the furniture around my head.

Like mothers to be having a shower
Or a new housekeeping trying too hard to impress,

They are horseflies that settle, get twitched,
Twizzz off.

Where has my peace of mind gone?
I need to paint the barn.

Maybe I will wear a dress when nobody's looking,
But no.

GREEN HEIGHTS

Ok. So here you are
In the anthology of the forgotten and damned
Like Hephaestus, like Lucifer
Eating a lime Italian ice.
It's documented you got where you are
For adoring God more than man.

True. You made mistakes: some doozies.
You left your wife and son one day
When a strong wind blew them across the horizon,
And blew you back into the bar
And drowned out their faces with absinthe,
Till your last dollar was in the till.

True. We made a mess of life
And left those who loved us for skanky solace —
Talked down into this basement:
Upswept, ungarnished, where white flickering
Candles flash on the gypsy's face
As open and pale as all of truth itself.

THE SPEAKER HAS THE HOUSE

Don't pay any attention
To this wild dance
Or my trying to steal the moon
From the dark sky and clench
It in a headlock, so never again
Will it make people so alone.

I have been in my room too long.
I have learned methods of avoiding madness.
The healers learn to make the unclean
Spic and Span again.

But I am disrespected.
It's not like I expect a rose carpet
Or a banner and brass section.

Something, just some slight something
To distinguish me from the commoner madman.

MUCH LESS FORGIVEN

And they had your nose to redden,
Laughing at a joke not meant to be funny —
Ha. Ha. Ha. A twelve-point buck in the bed.

That sorta stuff — the proof of your woodland soul.
Nowhere to hide when they come looking and
The golden sheen of rain on the roads at night

When you're taking the curves too fast.
It's not beyond reckoning you have a death wish.
All the bullies who stuffed you in a locker

Make as if they are your friends,
But you remember
Second bell in a rural hell.

PERSONALITY BY COMMITTEE

I see you — stretching out the years,
Putting red glitter polish on your toe nails,
Swatting at the flies of less than perfection,

In the dust the sparrows flicker
Like you and your destiny's playful effervescence.
The true you are many coy in the tank.

Everything matters and is part of a story,
Which can't be revealed
Like you in your bathing suit.

I like the way you punctuate when you talk.
It's crisp like breaking glass.
Or duller, duller than glass, I used the wrong word

LETTING THE SHADE UP

Lost between the pages
You find yourself in these shared
Moments almost wishing I would just
Disappear into the patterns.
Everyone seems like a fly strip.

You, one of few, catch a patterning
In all these goings on. Who am I
To chart your breadth and heartbeats?
Many people wish I would go away
Instead of jogging through these made midnights

In the rain covertly laughing.
Holding hands starts me thinking this way.
In this life of letters it's hard
To reconcile the you I know
With the you in all those paisley swatches.

TODAY'S MAIL

Carefree and comely
Is how I remember you best
When you took me out to make rounds
Of all the vintage clothing stores.

"Tell me. Be honest," you said
Holding up a tea-stained wedding dress,
And we laughed both because it was too large
And because we had been talking

About everyone getting engaged
"Won't catch me in one of these," you said.
And from what I hear you stuck to your guns.
I see you now in magazine roped in pearls

In dresses you can probably afford now.
I think of how good you always were with children,
You're living the life you wanted.
To think, all this sparked by a post card.

THREE CENTS WORTH

The river laughs and eddies all round
Your fine lines. The tips of the pines bristle
In the nervous calm. The gold pears are boxed.
This is not a gender thing understand.

Despite the weather, which by the way is gorgeous,
You stay indoors — wary of your fans.
I'm totally with you.
Fame brings torment in its basket.

Once you could fly and drive like normal people.
Fame and her escort of sundry anxieties,
Even the glimmer of generalized anxiety.
Sucks it victim into a lonely mansion

Where the blood runs — that's about it. It runs.
And you must be constantly be adjusted.
The blood pumped through your heart is brackish
Like a metaphor that can't bear its own weight.

EVIDENT COURAGE

The upstairs occupants would blacken my eyes.
My green eyes: my greener the money eyes.
They canvass someone to wipe the floor with me.

But I hide here in the sky. It's always scary
Me dreading morbid dread. People don't want to do
Stuff — normal everyday social stuff — with me.

The flag of my country is colorless.
I wear the crown of the King of Nowhere.
My citizens have all fled from under my reign.

And what if someone should want to assassinate me
In a bulletproof sedan without a driver.
What then?

DUCK BLIND BOURBON

You might be this or that.
Who is to say? Sheep or goat
Or pagan on this day.

I won't do that anymore —
Sure as a sycamore.

As certain as a charted storm,
You champion forgiveness,
But if it gets down to brass tacks,
You'll hold it against me

As certain as these clichés spit
At people — even friends. Take slander
To heart and fall into my shadow.

Swish go the skirts on the Avenues,
Like palms the children have in hand.
We are blind.

TOPS

The ceiling for pleasure
Is much higher here with you
Stretched alongside.

In the distortion, you become
A speckled mare eating
The apples I offer.

"No," you say and turn away
Toward a window of endless honeymoons,
And I take it at your word

As the congregation laughs a laughter
Dissolving as the sermon's ends.

A SHORT DRIVE

But it is not a sole peak, rising
But a range of risings

And musing. You put your life
In reverse instead of the now.

I have faith it all will be happy again —
Lighten this palate of somber tones.

That's part why I like you —
You turn my Rembrandt into Vermeer,

Cut stones and golden coins —
Walking around the red slip vases,

You, who still showed this morning
And despite the rain hopped the 4 train

Uptown and up the wet steps
While the wind tore wildly at your scarf.

INCIDENTAL MUSIC

Does he mean by this
That if one does not use the tool
That it will lose its edge — ?

Its power to carve and shape
Even the softest of woods:
Driftwood, for instance?

Gather yer gumballs while you may.
Tap the tallest maple, squash the grubs
That dot the parking lot

Of the school that raised you by accident
Into a man spray painting tags
And mixing tones on such a paper panel

Renewing itself like a lizard's tail —
Line after line —
Gauging success with an applause meter.

THE LONG AND SHORT OF IT

Mr. X is bald and gets what he wants
Save a full head of hair new set of teeth.
I am looking for new digs:
City or town — a rainy village under thatch.

Anywhere. I am broadcasting from a basement:
A shabby, illegal underground scab
Where it's my job to keep the furnace going
And check the oil gauge weekly.

These are not details I made up.
I mmmmmust be a real person writing these words.
Yet I confess only the most banal,
Most commonplace aspects of a sad life.

I hear it knocking now — the furnace, the brown
Bubbles coursing through the pipes. They are
The color of the coffee I buy each morning at the deli.
Sleep balks and rubs the ceiling like a balloon.

MOUNTING TOIL

Everything and nothing to do
Except iron his morning shirt. This came to him

In a dream when he should have been at work
In the office or the field.

I monitor surveillance screens so I know. I catch
Snippets of my love all about town.

I try not to look, but my colleague elbows me,
Draws my attention to the particular screen.

Seen and unseen my dove flies the field.
In the canting rain, which falls on rich and poor,

My love dissolves and reappears in the white phlox .
I can no longer isolate her from the rest.

THE ZOO

The monitor is on fire.
The way you and I take in
The drippings of fat in the blue flames!

They use us — again and again.
They would have us believe
It is still light out.

The organ plays through the pipes
When it is lightening outside.
The rain tells the truth.

Heaven is nearer
Than heaven — a shoulder
That can almost bear our weight.

THE BOYS ABOVE ARE BAFFLED

The words are there, but they are dampened
By the ceiling, which allows but little
Of the anger to pass through the tiles.

We try to live a good life.
Sure, we've made mistakes.
Who hasn't? But as the larger picture
Emerges from the points and pixels,

An urgency to do better emerges.
Some of the fruit went sour, but overall
The relevant trees yielded bountiful sweet

Harvest, in my and your own lifetime.

SIMPLE PLEASURES

I admit it falls on me — the haven
Of blame sudden as a sneeze,
But I was minding my pleasure in the trees
When everyone was looking at the ground.

X can be a ton of fun, but Y is born of a dryer
Humor — more appeal to age, to those
Who have given up the search for meaning.
But really — no one ever really gives up hope.

The batteries in my flashlight are dying.
Still, I search in the darkness for that picture
You drew as a youthful diversion
To trace out the memory of a garden to be.

AFTER LONG SUFFERING

The sound is not random. It is part —
Or imparted — design. Cheers! You are back again

Combing your hair in the silver
Mirror that once had in mind your rich color.

Your original dark succumbed with time
And the trauma of a failed marriage that carved

A pair of initials in the loving onset
Into the rippling bark of an oak.

Such was a wound turned scar ever darkening —
Like the storm clouds churning over you,

Skimming the edge of sense and broken vows
That helped the pilot back into his ship.

OFF THE GROUND, BUT BARELY

I admitted I hadn't returned the picture,
But you had told me to hold onto it.
It wasn't intentional like pines planted in row
Or the wild turns you made in the snow.

We shared the life oak bordering St. Charles Ave,
Which makes me think of those who came before.
Before us — and who had passed on quietly
Each with consideration of the other.

Of course, no children were involved.
That's a real game changer. We are forever involved —
Forever tied by our love for our son,
Who makes it worth it — seeing him

Grow so quickly from infant to super hero
Into what and who he is always becoming.
Civil, amicable, or hostile: the jet streams above
Bring our words back to earth again.

OFFERING OF DISTRACTION

It took some convincing.
On that much you agree. I'm sorry —
But making out in the laundromat
Isn't my idea of the perfect date.

You get huffy: "Well then, YOU fold it.
I'm going home." But we talk it out, about
A suit of armor from the 14th century
We had seen earlier and the Post-War

Search for an aesthetic. We dragged on
Into the possibility of dental school.
We still, as yet, have hope between us.
I am set on trying this…listening.

VARIOUS ENCLOSURES

The shy are ushered into the hollow
Hall. Each door is numbered.
Early on, you were of their count and coven.
One crow was always calling,
Which, you alone, noticed — you alone
Found yourself here, where the lines are cast
And the nets are thrown to bring you in.

YOUR TURN

This is the thanks you get
For teaching your shadow
To shake hands with my shadow.

In the evening a penumbra forms —
Rock, paper, scissors.
The moon is blind, or rather

Dumb, unable to say
Anything about our union.
The tears fall into your palm

Simply because you hold it out.
Asking is part of receiving,
And the rain is always a stranger.

BLUE LIGHTHOUSE

Time changes the living —
Even the inanimate waves in the sand
Are scooped and used to fill this hourglass,

And you and your redwoods — a canopy
Cast mottled patches of blurred light,
Wave and particle at such height.

The stethoscope holds a secret
The doctor keeps buried in his charts.
It is not always best to know your prognosis.

And the beach trees shadow
The gray Trident submarines of your thoughts,
And the waves turn silently toward sweet oblivion

YOUR CARRYALL BAG

You take your colored marker
And color in the feathers of a red bird.

They are arguing upstairs. You know
Who's who by their voice and temper.

The mother speaks into oblivion.
The children are left to carve the silence.

This all was written in a college ruled notebook.
That is why the lines are the way they are.

When I am done, I will type them in
With hopes the red bird will fly away.

RED STRINGER

You father showed you how to skip a stone
Across the old mill pond. They sank at first,
But the overture of the wind in the pines
Inspired a gradual knowledge how to make them skitter.

But why are we talking about this?
Why are we talking about this at all?
Those stoves are in alluvial sludge.
They will, like your youth, never be recovered.

And yet the machine goes on out of obsession
Talking, talking nostalgia through the dripping.
Through the sieve, memory sifts down.
You are growing sleepy. You are growing very sleepy.

LISTING BREEZE

A quiet afternoon in your bathroom
With the rain pinging on the tin roof.
It's mainly a mood thing. We talk quietly
In the English which you are learning.

Raindrops, peace of mind, your curves
And your knees rise
Through the white suds and Epson salts —
If only people knew this you.

FLYING ON ETHER

How can you not wipe her tears?
They were patented by the office of heartbreak.
Now. Seeing her face for the first time
While words blow through these pages like rainbows.

"You will never know me now," you say. "Never."
"You will not catch and pin my soul down
Like one of your silly butterflies you keep
And take out of that dovetail box these warm nights…"

It was true. She was off in the head.
Her last husband warned me making
A cuckoo sign at his left ear.

But I hold a place for the singular:
The victims of the mockingbird syndrome,
And all the damned dear.

GROWTH OF AN ENGLISH BOXWOOD

These are just shadows through the screen
In a omniscient summer dusk, when
The only horizon's you like catch a glimpse of
Is the haven of the player's green room.

And I am not one to gainsay
The figures you say are real are real.
In other farther countries of the globe
You will always carry my silent prayers.

You go making it through your private darkness,
If only on a notebook page, here and now.

ANOTHER BASSOON TRACK

This is the room where winners break.
Break bad. This is the room of chalk.
This is the land of blue-chalked cues.

You were taken out in the first round.
You never had even this much of a chance.

So you ordered a Mexican beer and a shot
Of the cheapest well tequila in the house.

Listen. Nobody here really knows you
But there are worse things
Than being misunderstood.

Take it from one who knows.
Take it from your new haircut.

Take it from the way
Everyone seems to be slurring their words —
Except for you, except you in your silence.

MEBANE ROBERTSON, was born in 1967 in Lynchburg, Virginia, and raised in Richmond, Virginia. He attended and graduated from The College of William and Mary with a B.A. After spending a few years in New Orleans, he moved to Brooklyn and eventually earned his Ph.D. in English at Fordham University. Along the way, he both taught and tutored mostly as an adjunct professor. After writing and immersing himself in poetry and music since his teenage years, his first book *Signal from Draco* was published in 2007. While writing the poems that would appear in *An American Unconscious,* he pursued interests in both fiction writing and songwriting.

TITLES FROM BLACK WIDOW PRESS
TRANSLATION SERIES

A Life of Poems, Poems of a Life
by Anna de Noailles. Translated by Norman
R. Shapiro. Introduction by Catherine Perry.

Approximate Man and Other Writings
by Tristan Tzara. Translated and edited
by Mary Ann Caws.

Art Poétique by Guillevic.
Translated by Maureen Smith.

The Big Game by Benjamin Péret. Translated
with an introduction by Marilyn Kallet.

*Boris Vian Invents Boris Vian:
A Boris Vian Reader.*
Edited and translated by Julia Older.

Capital of Pain by Paul Eluard.
Translated by Mary Ann Caws,
Patricia Terry, and Nancy Kline.

Chanson Dada: Selected Poems by Tristan Tzara.
Translated with an introduction and essay by
Lee Harwood.

*Essential Poems and Writings of Joyce Mansour:
A Bilingual Anthology.* Translated with an
introduction by Serge Gavronsky.

Essential Poems and Prose of Jules Laforgue.
Translated and edited by Patricia Terry.

*Essential Poems and Writings of Robert Desnos:
A Bilingual Anthology.* Edited with an
introduction and essay by Mary Ann Caws.

EyeSeas (Les Ziaux) by Raymond Queneau.
Translated with an introduction by Daniela
Hurezanu and Stephen Kessler.

Fables in a Modern Key by Pierre Coran.
Edited and translated by Norman R. Shapiro.
Full-color illustrations by Olga Pastuchiv.

*Forbidden Pleasures: New Selected Poems
1924–1949* by Luis Cernuda. Translated by
Stephen Kessler.

Furor and Mystery & Other Writings
by René Char. Edited and translated
by Mary Ann Caws and Nancy Kline.

*Guarding the Air:
Selected Poems of Gunnar Harding.*
Translated and edited by Roger Greenwald.

The Inventor of Love & Other Writings
by Gherasim Luca. Translated by Julian & Laura
Semilian. Introduction by Andrei Codrescu.
Essay by Petre Răileanu.

Jules Supervielle: Selected Prose and Poetry.
Translated by Nancy Kline and Patricia Terry.

La Fontaine's Bawdy by Jean de La Fontaine.
Translated with an introduction by
Norman R. Shapiro.

Last Love Poems of Paul Eluard.
Translated with an introduction by
Marilyn Kallet.

Love, Poetry (L'amour la poésie) by Paul Eluard.
Translated with an essay by Stuart Kendall.

Pierre Reverdy: Poems, Early to Late.
Translated by Mary Ann Caws and
Patricia Terry.

Poems of André Breton: A Bilingual Anthology.
Translated with essays by Jean-Pierre Cauvin
and Mary Ann Caws.

Poems of A.O. Barnabooth by Valery Larbaud.
Translated by Ron Padgett and Bill Zavatsky.

Poems of Consummation by Vicente Aleixandre.
Translated by Stephen Kessler.

Préversities: A Jacques Prévert Sampler.
Translated and edited by Norman R. Shapiro.

The Sea and Other Poems by Guillevic.
Translated by Patricia Terry. Introduction by
Monique Chefdor.

To Speak, to Tell You? Poems by Sabine Sicaud.
Translated by Norman R. Shapiro. Intro-
duction and notes by Odile Ayral-Clause.

Forthcoming Translations

Earthlight (Clair de Terre)
by André Breton. Translated by Bill Zavatsky
and Zack Rogrow. (New and revised edition.)

*The Gentle Genius of Cécile Périn:
Selected Poems (1906–1956).*
Edited and translated by Norman R. Shapiro.

MODERN POETRY SERIES

ABC of Translation by Willis Barnstone

An Alchemist with One Eye on Fire
by Clayton Eshleman

An American Unconscious by Mebane Robertson

Anticline by Clayton Eshleman

Archaic Design by Clayton Eshleman

Backscatter: New and Selected Poems
by John Olson

Barzakh (Poems 2000–2012) by Pierre Joris

The Caveat Onus by Dave Brinks

City Without People: The Katrina Poems
by Niyi Osundare

Clayton Eshleman/The Essential Poetry:
1960–2015

Concealments and Caprichos
by Jerome Rothenberg

Crusader-Woman by Ruxandra Cesereanu.
Translated by Adam J. Sorkin. Introduction
by Andrei Codrescu.

Curdled Skulls: Poems of Bernard Bador.
Translated by Bernard Bador with
Clayton Eshleman.

Disenchanted City (La ville désenchantée)
by Chantal Bizzini. Edited by Marilyn Kallet
and J. Bradford Anderson. Translated by
J. Bradford Anderson, Darren Jackson, and
Marilyn Kallet.

Endure: Poems by Bei Dao. Translated by
Clayton Eshleman and Lucas Klein.

Exile Is My Trade: A Habib Tengour Reader.
Translated by Pierre Joris.

Eye of Witness: A Jerome Rothenberg Reader.
Edited with commentaries by Heriberto Yepez
& Jerome Rothenberg.

Fire Exit by Robert Kelly

Forgiven Submarine
by Ruxandra Cesereanu and Andrei Codrescu

from stone this running by Heller Levinson

The Grindstone of Rapport:
A Clayton Eshleman Reader

Larynx Galaxy by John Olson

The Love That Moves Me by Marilyn Kallet

Memory Wing by Bill Lavender

Packing Light: New and Selected Poems
by Marilyn Kallet

The Present Tense of the World: Poems 2000–2009
by Amina Saïd. Translated with an introduction
by Marilyn Hacker.

The Price of Experience by Clayton Eshleman

The Secret Brain: Selected Poems 1995–2012
by Dave Brinks

Signal from Draco: New and Selected Poems
by Mebane Robertson

Soraya (Sonnets) by Anis Shivani

Wrack Lariat by Heller Levinson

Forthcoming Modern Poetry Titles

Funny Way of Staying Alive by Willis Barnstone

The Hexagon by Robert Kelly

Memory by Bernadette Mayer

LITERARY THEORY / BIOGRAPHY SERIES

Barbaric Vast & Wild: A Gathering of Outside
and Subterranean Poetry (*Poems for the*
Millennium, v. 5) Eds: Jerome Rothenberg
and John Bloomberg-Rissman

Clayton Eshleman: The Whole Art
by Stuart Kendall

Revolution of the Mind: The Life of André Breton
by Mark Polizzotti

WWW.BLACKWIDOWPRESS.COM